THE CANADIAN PRESS

CAPS and SPELLING

19th EDITION
Fully revised and updated

Patti Tasko, Ed.

THE CANADIAN PRESS
36 King St. East, Toronto, Ontario M5C 2L9

www.thecanadianpress.com

Library and Archives Canada Cataloguing in Publication

The Canadian Press caps and spelling. -- 19th ed.

Edited by Patti Tasko.
ISBN 978-0-920009-44-4

1. English language--Capitalization. 2. English
language--Orthography and spelling. I. Tasko, Patti
II. Canadian Press III. Title: Caps and spelling.

PE1450.C72 2009   423'.1   C2009-900365-1

First printing 1965 Revised 1969, 1973, 1976, 1978, 1981, 1985,
1986, 1987, 1988, 1990, 1992, 1996, 1998, 2000, 2003, 2005, 2007
and 2009.

Design and cover art by
Sean Vokey
The Canadian Press

Foreword

With this edition, The Canadian Press has now issued its *Caps and Spelling* guide 19 times. Over the 44-year life of *Caps*, the entries that have been added, dropped or changed provide a revealing window into the writing and editing concerns of Canadian journalism.

The first edition, in 1965, had listings for A-bomb and H-bomb, Trans-Canada Air Lines, the British Empire Games, Eskimo and Viet Nam in its 46 pages. By 1969 the book had grown to 94 pages, the British Empire Games had become the Commonwealth Games and Viet Nam, Vietnam. New entries included hippie, Bobby Gimby's centennial song *Ca-na-da* and Irish hospitals sweepstakes, a 1960s precursor to today's government-run lotteries.

Twelve years later, in 1981, the book was recommending Inuk and Inuit instead of Eskimo and also had listings for such well-known newsmakers as Dr. Henry Morgentaler and Menachem Begin.

And on it has gone. Seventies game-show personality Monty Hall is dropped; today's TV personality George Stroumboulopoulos is added. The Dominion Bureau of Statistics becomes Statistics Canada. Oriental (for race) becomes Asian.

Some references, however, found in the first edition are still with us today. Canadian writers still need to know it's Timiskaming in Ontario but Témiscaming in Quebec, grey (not gray), and Confederation, not confederation.

And the goal of the first edition is still the goal of the 19th — to bring together the proper names and abbreviations most likely to cause problems for those handling copy in Canadian newsrooms.

Foreword

In this edition, many listings have been updated or removed and new ones added, including: Leona Aglukkaq, Afrocentric, airstrike, BC Ferries, BC Hydro, Rod Bruinooge, Canwest, coastline, coed, Craigslist, crossover, CUV, do-not-call list, DVR, ER, Fundamentalist Church of Jesus Christ of Latter Day Saints, G-force, GlaxoSmithKline, *Guitar Hero*, handgun, Harris-Decima, headdress, hijinks, hoodie, HPV, Humvee, Hummer, IED, IPO, Michaëlle Jean, knuckleball, landline, Listeria, listeriosis, log in, login, mill rate, model, Mount Sinai Hospital, NASCAR, Ontario Teachers' Pension Plan, pixel, pixelate, polygamist, polygamous, pompom, rendezvous, Rio Tinto Alcan, roundtable, RSS, SEAL, smartphone, spam, sports writer, storyteller, storytelling, subtrade, tax-free savings account, text message, Ticketmaster, timeline, transgender, Veterans Affairs Canada, Wi-LAN Inc., World Trade Center, write down and writedown.

This edition has also been updated to reflect style changes made with the publication of the 15th edition of the *Canadian Press Stylebook* in 2008. We now follow an organization's capitalization for trade names and other proper names, with two exceptions: we capitalize only the first letter of all-caps and all-lowercase promotional names. So it is now eBay and iPod, not Ebay and IPod. Some specific exceptions, for readability, may be necessary; they will be listed in this book. And we have dropped the hyphen from email, although other such constructions (e-commerce) maintain it.

Also in the list of changes, we are now abbreviating senator and representative before people's names: Sen. Nancy Greene, Sen. John McCain, Rep. John Smith. Iles de la Madeleine didn't have hyphens when it was just an island but is now Iles-de-la-Madeleine to reflect its status as a Quebec municipality. The Stratford Shakespeare Festival now is the official name of what used to be the Stratford Festival. Premier is now officially to be used for leaders of Canadian territories. And Detroit Three is preferred to Big Three (except in historical references) to describe GM, Ford and Chrysler, as they are no longer the largest automakers.

This 19th edition is also the first we have built online. Both *Caps* and the *Stylebook* now are available online, and subscribers to the Internet version have already received the updates and additions in this book. If you are interested in real-time updates and email notifications of all style changes or additional content in our books, visit thecanadianpress.com/ books.

Many of the changes and additions to *Caps and Spelling* come at the request of the writers and editors who use the *Canadian Press Stylebook* and this book. Thanks go to those alert and loyal users who help keep this reference up to date.

Patti Tasko, Editor

patti.tasko@thecanadianpress.com

Capitalization

1. The Canadian Press follows a modified down style. This is the basic rule:

Capitalize all proper names, the names of departments and agencies of national and provincial governments, trade names, names of associations, companies, clubs, religions, languages, races, places, addresses. Otherwise, lowercase is favoured where a reasonable option exists.

2. Common nouns — church, league — are capitalized when part of a proper name: Anglican Church, National Hockey League. They are normally lowercased when standing alone: the church's stand, a league spokesman.

3. The common-noun elements of proper nouns are normally lowercase in plural uses: the United and Anglican churches, the National and American leagues.

4. Formal titles directly preceding a name are capitalized: Prime Minister Jean Chrétien, Archbishop Aloysius Ambrozic. They are lowercased standing alone and in plural uses: the prime minister, the archbishop, premiers Jean Charest and Ralph Klein.

5. As a rule of thumb, formal titles are those that are almost an integral part of a person's name — they could be used with the surname alone, if that were Canadian Press style: Ald. Cowan, Rabbi Steinberg, Sgt. Duplessis.

6. Job descriptions are lowercased: soprano Maria Stratas, managing editor Anne Davies, Acme Corp. chairman Joseph Schultz.

7. Long or cumbersome titles and job descriptions

should be set off with commas: Jean Dubois, energy, mines and resources minister, attended. Or: The energy, mines and resources minister, Jean Dubois, attended. An internationally known Canadian architect, Arthur Erickson, was present.

8. All references to the current Pope, Canada's reigning monarch and the current Governor General are capitalized.

9. Titles of nobility, religion and suchlike that are commonly used instead of the personal name are capitalized: Duke of Kent, Anglican Primate of Canada. But the duke, the primate.

10. The names of national legislative bodies, including some short forms, are capitalized: House of Commons, the House, the Commons; U.S. Senate; Knesset. Provincial legislatures and local councils are lowercased: Quebec national assembly, Toronto city council.

11. National and provincial government departments and agencies are capitalized: Health Canada, Defence Department, Ministry of Natural Resources, U.S. Secret Service. Local government departments and boards are lowercased: parks and property department, Halifax welfare department.

12. Upper courts are capitalized: B.C. Supreme Court, Appeal Court. Lower courts are lowercased: juvenile court, magistrate's court.

13. Canada's military forces are capitalized: Canadian Forces, the Forces. For other forces, army, navy and air force are lowercased when preceded by the name of the country: the Greek air force, the U.S. army. This style is intended for consistency since the proper name is not always a combination of country

and force: the Royal Navy, the British navy; the Royal Air Force, the British air force.

14. Historical periods, historic events, holy days and other special times are capitalized: Middle Ages, First World War, Prohibition, Christmas Eve, Ramadan, Earth Day, October Crisis.

15. Specific geographical regions and features are capitalized: Western Canada, Far North, Lake Superior, Niagara Peninsula. But northern, southern, eastern and western in terms derived from regions are lowercased: a western Canadian, a southerner, northern customs.

16. Regions not generally known as specific geographical areas are lowercase: southern Ontario, eastern Alberta, northern Newfoundland.

17. Sacred names and the proper names and nicknames of the devil are capitalized: the Almighty, Redeemer, Holy Spirit, Allah, Mother of God, Vishnu, Beelzebub, Father of Lies. But devil, hell and heaven are lowercased.

18. Names of races, nations and the like are capitalized: Aboriginal Peoples, Asian, Arab, French-Canadian. But white and black are lowercased.

19. The principal words of titles of books, plays, movies, paintings and the like are capitalized: *A Dictionary of Usage and Style, Androcles and the Lion, Gone With the Wind, Isle of the Dead*. Principal words are nouns, pronouns, adjectives, adverbs, verbs, the first and last word of the title, as well as prepositions and conjunctions of four letters or more. For infinitives, use to Go, to Be. Both words of compound adjectives are capitalized: Well-Meaning.

20. Nicknames and fanciful names are capitalized: Speedy Gonzales, Mack the Knife, Third World, Group of Seven.

21. Awards and decorations are capitalized: Order of Canada, OC; Victoria Cross, VC. University degrees are lowercased except when abbreviated: master of arts, a master's, MA; doctor of philosophy, PhD.

22. Proper nouns and adjectives now regarded as common nouns are lowercased: brussels sprouts, french fries, draconian, scotch.

23. Except in the cases of all-lowercase or all-uppercase names, follow the capitalization used by the organization or person unless it hampers readability: eBay, iPod, WestJet, k.d. lang. Note: Capitalize at the beginning of a sentence: EBay. If a corporate or promotional name is all lowercase, cap the first letter for clarity: Adidas. If the name is all uppercase, cap only the first letter for readability: Band-Aid (not BAND-AID). Some exceptions to these rules may be necessary for readability; they will be listed in this book.

For a fuller treatment of capitalization, see the Canadian Press Stylebook, chapter Capitalization.

Spelling

1. The *Canadian Oxford Dictionary* is the authority for Canadian Press spelling with specific exceptions noted in the *Canadian Press Stylebook* and this guide. Where optional forms are given — moustache, mustache — the first listed is Canadian Press style.

2. When the spelling of the common-noun element of a proper name differs from Canadian Press style — Center Harbor, N.H., Lincoln Center, Canadian Paediatric Society — use the spelling favoured by the subject. One exception is names of government departments and agencies. Use U.S. Defence (not Defense) Department and U.S. Labour (not Labor) Department to avoid inconsistency with other words likely to be found in the story, such as defence secretary and labour legislation.

3. The Canadian Press ignores symbols and unnecessary punctuation in corporate or other names or translates them into accepted punctuation if necessary: 'N Sync, not *NSYNC; the Bravo TV channel, not Bravo!; Mamma Mia, not Mamma Mia! Check individual listings.

4. Canadian Press style is -our, not -or, for labour, honour and other such words of more than one syllable in which the "u" is not pronounced:

arbour	ardour	armour
behaviour	candour	clamour
clangour	colour	demeanour
discolour	dishonour	enamour
endeavour	favour	fervour
flavour	glamour	harbour
honour	humour	labour
neighbour	odour	parlour
rancour	rigour	rumour
saviour	savour	splendour

tumour   valour   vapour
vigour

5. In some forms of these words, however, the "u" is dropped, especially when an -ous ending is added: laborious, rancorous, odorous, honorary.

6. Canadian Press style also reflects "Canadian" spellings that are different from American spellings. Some examples (American form in brackets):

axe (ax)	catalogue (catalog)
centre (center)	cheque (check)
defence (defense)	enrol (enroll)
grey (gray)	ketchup (catsup)
licence (n.) (license)	litre (liter)
manoeuvre (maneuver)	meagre (meager)
metre (meter)	mould (mold)
moustache (mustache)	offence (offense)
pedlar (peddler)	skilful (skillful)
sombre (somber)	spectre (specter)
syrup (sirup)	theatre (theater)
pyjamas (pajamas)	

As well, Canadian Press and Canadian style is usually to double the l when adding endings to words such as label and signal. American spelling tends to leave it as a single l.

7. For words in common use, Canadian Press style is simple "e" rather than the diphthongs "ae" and "oe." Thus Canadian Press style is archeologist, ecumenical, encyclopedia, esthetic, fetus, gynecologist, hemorrhage, medieval, paleontologist, pedagogy and pediatrician.

8. Generally, proper names retain the diphthong: Caesar, Oedipus, Phoebe. Also hors d'oeuvre, manoeuvre and subpoena. The "ae" in aerial, aerate and such is considered normal spelling.

Spelling

9. The umlaut — ä, ö and ü — in German names is indicated by the letter "e" after the letter affected. Thus: Goering for Göring.

10. The -ov and -ev endings for Russian names are used instead of -off and -eff. Exceptions include such familiar names as Rachmaninoff, Smirnoff and Ignatieff, where the spelling is established.

11. Canadian Press style for First Nations names is to follow the preference of the band. For a current list of bands and their preferred spellings, check the Publications and Research page (community profiles) on the website of the Department of Indian and Northern Affairs (www.inac.gc.ca).

12. For Arabic names, use an English spelling that approximates the way a name sounds in Arabic. If an individual has a preferred spelling in English, use it.

13. Use the Ukrainian, not the Russian, transliteration for Ukrainian place names: Chornobyl (not Chernobyl); Kyiv (not Kiev).

Abbreviations

1. All-capital abbreviations are written without periods (YMCA, AFL-CIO, CN, MP, URL, RIP,) unless the abbreviation is geographical (U.S., B.C., P.E.I., T.O., U.K.) refers to a person (J.R. Ewing) or is a single letter (N. for north but NNW).

2. Most lowercase and mixed abbreviations take periods: f.o.b., Jr., Ont., No., B.Comm.

3. Mixed abbreviations that begin and end with a capital letter do not take periods: PhD, PoW, U of T.

4. Acronyms — abbreviations pronounced as words — formed from only the first letter of each principal word are all capitals: AIDS (acquired immune deficiency syndrome), NATO (North Atlantic Treaty Organization), NOW (National Organization for Women).

5. In most cases, acronyms formed from initial and other letters are upper and lowercase: Dofasco (Dominion Foundries and Steel Corp.), Nabisco (National Biscuit Co.), Norad (North American Aerospace Defence Command). Some exceptions have crept into common use (BMO, for Bank of Montreal); check individual listings.

6. Acronyms that have become common words are not capitalized: laser (light amplification by stimulated emission of radiation), radar (radio detection and ranging).

7. Metric symbols are not abbreviations and do not take periods: m, l, kW.

8. Plurals are MPs and PoWs; possessives MPs' and PoWs'.

9. Most abbreviations are written without spaces: U.K., W.Va., P.Eng. But those written without periods

Abbreviations

are spaced: U of T.

10. Ampersands are allowed if used as part of a corporate name: A&W, Standard & Poor's, and in expressions like R&B. Usually, these are written without spaces when all-capital abbreviations are used and with spaces when they are not. Check individual listings.

See also the Canadian Press Stylebook, chapter Abbreviations and acronyms.

Compounds, Hyphens

1. Compound words may be written solid (website), open (oil rig) or hyphenated (yo-yo). Style is usually determined by the most common usage. A new compound is normally written at first as two or more words, becomes increasingly hyphenated and finally is combined into one word.

2. For compound words, follow the *Canadian Oxford Dictionary* unless the listing in this book differs. If the word is not listed in either, write it as separate words.

3. For compound modifiers, in general hyphenate when preceding a noun, but not if the meaning is instantly clear because of common usage of the term: three-under-par 69 *but* sales tax increase.

4. Hyphens are seldom needed with proper nouns (a North American trend), established foreign terms (a 10 per cent increase) or established compound nouns (a high school teacher).

5. Certain word combinations are often hyphenated even when standing alone: noun plus adjective (fire-resistant); noun plus participle (blood-stained); adjective plus participle (hard-earned); adjective plus noun (red-faced).

6. Hyphenate most well-known compounds of three words: happy-go-lucky; three-year-old. But there are exceptions: coat of arms; next of kin; no man's land.

7. Use a hyphen to avoid doubling a vowel, tripling a consonant or duplicating a prefix: co-operate; doll-like; sub-subcommittee.

8. Use a hyphen to join prefixes to proper names: anti-Liberal; pro-Bush.

9. Use a hyphen to join an initial capital with a word:

Compounds, Hyphens

T-shirt; S-bend.

10. Use a hyphen to avoid awkward combinations of letters and to differentiate words: correspondent (letter writer) *but* co-respondent (in court); resign (quit) *but* re-sign (sign again).

11. Use a hyphen for the minus sign in temperatures and in bracketed political affiliations: -10 degrees; Donna Hooper (Con-Ont.)

For more information on compound words and hyphens, see the Canadian Press Stylebook, chapters Compound Words and Punctuation.

Place Names

1. National Geographic Society spellings are Canadian Press style for place names outside Canada with exceptions listed in the *Canadian Press Stylebook* and this guide.

2. The style authority for Canadian place names is the *Canadian Oxford Dictionary*, with some exceptions listed in this guide. If the place name is not in *Oxford*, consult the Secretariat of the Canadian Permanent Committee on Geographical Names (http://geonames.nrcan.gc.ca). For French place names, see next page.

French Capitalization

1. For the French names of organizations and the titles of books, songs, plays, movies, paintings and the like, The Canadian Press prefers the English form for the sake of readability: Quebec Liquor Corp., not Société des alcools du Québec; Remembrance of Things Past, not A la recherche du temps perdu.

2. In general, when the French name or title is used (in a quotation, for example) it should be followed by a description in English or a translation: Office de la langue française, or the government language agency; Le Malade imaginaire (The Imaginary Invalid).

3. If a work, organization or the like is commonly known by its French name, it need not be followed by a translation: La Bohème, Notre Dame, Le Droit.

4. The names of some organizations cannot really be translated (Conseil du patronat, the largest employer group in Quebec), or have become familiar in their French version (the Ecole polytechnique, the engineering school), or have no official English version (the Centrale des syndicats du Québec, the union that represents teachers).

5. The Canadian Press uses hyphens in multi-word French place names in Quebec and abroad: Trois-Rivières, Ste-Anne-de-Beaupré, Stanstead-Est, Ver-sur-Mer. Hyphens are omitted from purely English place names: Stanstead Plain, and if the first word is not a place name but a natural feature: Lac Barrière, Baie des Chaleurs.

6. For the names of saints (except in place names) use St. (not Ste.) for female as well as male: St. Dorothee.

7. French dictionaries used by The Canadian Press are *Le Petit Robert* and *Le Petit Larousse*.

French Capitalization

8. For the names of organizations, the first word is capitalized unless it is an article; other words except proper nouns are lowercase: (le) Service de perception, Emballages St-Laurent ltée.

9. For the titles of books, songs and the like, the first word is capitalized — the second too when the first is an article — and proper nouns: De la terre à la lune, Sur le pont d'Avignon, Les Liaisons dangereuses.

10. For the names of newspapers, the definite article, the first noun and proper nouns are capitalized: Le Journal de Montréal, Le Courrier du peuple.

A

A, An—Use "a" before consonant sounds: a historic building, a university, a one-way ticket, a euphemism, a 1914 novel. Use "an" before vowel sounds: an apple, an honest man, an S-bend, an 1814 novel, an RRSP.

A&E (specialty TV channel)

A&W

Abbott, Sir John (prime minister, 1891-92)

ABC (acceptable in all references for American Broadcasting Cos. — note plural)

abhor, abhorrence, abhorrent

Abidjan

Abitibi-Consolidated Inc. (TSX:A)

able seaman (*no abbvn.*)

Ablonczy, Diane (politician)

abominable snowman (yeti)

aboriginal (*adj., n. when referring to individual*); in Australia: Aboriginal or Aborigine

Aboriginal Peoples (all of Canada's Indians, Inuit and Métis)

abscess

abysmal (*not* -ss-)

abyss

Academy of Motion Picture Arts and Sciences, the academy

Acadie nouvelle, L' (newspaper in Caraquet, N.B.)

accessible (*not* -able)

accommodate (-mm-), accommodation

acetaminophen

acetylene

acetylsalicylic acid (ASA)

Achilles heel, tendon

acknowledgment

acquit, acquitted, acquittal

Act—Capitalize titles of parliamentary acts but not subsequent references when the full name

is not used. And references to acts and bills
before royal assent are lowercase.
—Food and Drugs Act
—the food act says ...
—a proposed food act
acting, acting mayor James Borden, acting Sgt. Jane
   Bloom
Action démocratique du Québec (ADQ or Action
   démocratique *on second reference*)
actor (OK for both men and women)
ACTRA (Alliance of Canadian Cinema, Television
   and Radio Artists)
Act 3, Scene 2; the third act, second scene
AD—Acceptable in all references for anno Domini
   (in the year of the Lord). The abbreviation
   goes before the figure for the year: AD 410. It
   may also be used to refer to a century: the first
   century AD.
adaptability
addendum, addenda
Addresses—Capitalize Street, Road, etc., used
   with names; *but* King and Victoria streets.
   Abbreviate in addresses when the number is
   used; *but* 10 Downing Street, 24 Sussex Drive
   (official residences).
   —36 King St. E., Toronto M5C 2L9
   —the Portage Avenue bus
   —Wellington Crescent
   —Cres., Blvd., Rd., Sq.
Adidas (*not* adidas)
adieu, adieus
adjuster (*not* -or)
administration, U.S. administration
Admiral John Smith (*no abbvn.*)
   —the admiral said ...
admiralty

—the admiralty reported ...
—first lord of the admiralty
—the first lord's statement
—Admiralty Court
admissible (*not* -able), admissibility
ad nauseam (*not* -eum)
Adonai
adrenalin
Adventist, Seventh-day
adverse (unfavourable), averse (reluctant)
advertise (*not* -ize)
adviser (*not* -or)
aerial
aerodynamics
Aeroflot airline
Aeronautics Act
aesthetic — *Use* esthetic
affect (*v.,* have effect on)
affidavit
affront (deliberate insult), effrontery (shameless
        insolence)
Afghan (*n.* and *adj., prefer to* Afghani)
aficionado (*one f*), aficionados
AFL-CIO (acceptable in all references for American
        Federation of Labor-Congress of Industrial
        Organizations)
African-American
African Union (AU, *but avoid*)
Afrikaans (language)
Afrikaner (person)
Afrocentric (*not* Africentric)
Aga Khan, the
Agence France-Presse (AFP)
agenda, agendas
agent provocateur, agents provocateurs
aggression, aggressive

aging (*not* ageing)

Aglukark, Susan

Aglukkaq, Leona (federal health minister)

agreement

—a Canada-U.S. agreement on power

—General Agreement on Tariffs and Trade (GATT)

aide-de-camp, aides-de-camp

AIDS (for acquired immune deficiency syndrome)

airbag

airbase

Airbus

Air Canada (*no abbvn.*)

—ACE Aviation Holdings Inc. (parent company; TSX:ACE.B)

Air Commodore John Smith (*no abbvn.*)

—the air commodore said ...

Aircraft Names — Use a hyphen between symbols for the make or type and the model number.

—DC-8L, B-57, A-320, MiG-25, CF-18

—Yak-42, AN-154, IL-62, TU-144

—*but* Dash 8 (*no hyphen*)

aircrew (*one word*)

airdrop (*one word*)

Air Force—Capitalize air force in references to the pre-unification Royal Canadian Air Force. For other forces, lowercase air force when preceded by the name of the country.

—British air force

—Royal Air Force

—U.S. or American air force

—U.S. 8th Air Force

—the air force planes

—Bomber Command

—Fleet Air Arm

—126 Squadron

—the squadron headquarters are ...
Air India (*no hyphen*)
airlift (*n.* and *v.*)
Air Line Pilots Association (ALPA)
airmail (*n.* and *v.*)
airman (*no abbvn.*)
Air Marshal Lois Jones (*no abbvn.*)
    —the air marshal said ...
Air Miles (loyalty program)
Airport—Lowercase unless the official name is
    used.
    —Pearson International Airport
    —Toronto international airport
    —Vancouver International Airport
    —the Vancouver airport
airstrike (*one word*)
Air Vice-Marshal John Candy (*no abbvn.*)
    —the air vice-marshal
a.k.a.
Aklavik, N.W.T.
Akwesasne Mohawk Territory
Al—In Arabic names of individuals, the articles el
    and al may be used or dropped depending
    on the person's preference or established
    usage: Ayman al-Zawahri, al-Zawahri (*second
    reference*); *but* Moammar Gadhafi, Gadhafi.
  For other names, the article is usually uppercase:
    Al-Jazeera (Arab all-news satellite channel)
Alabama (Ala.)
Alaska (*no abbvn.*)
Alberta (Alta.)
Alberta Heritage Savings Trust Fund (*no abbvn.*)
Alcoholics Anonymous (AA)
    —Al-Anon (for relatives of alcoholics)
    —Alateen (for children of alcoholics)
alderman, alderwoman (Ald.)

—Ald. John Doe
—alderwomen Jill Jones and Julia Wong
Alderwoods Group Inc.
    — formerly Loewen Group Inc.
Alghabra, Omar (MP)
Algonquian (aboriginal language family)
Algonquin (Ojibwa dialect)
Allah
Allahu akbar! (God is great)
all-America (team), all-American (individual)
Allan Cup (hockey)
Alliance Atlantis Communications Inc.
    (TSX:AAC.B)
Alliance of Canadian Cinema, Television and Radio
    Artists (ACTRA)
Allied forces, the Allies (in world wars)
allophone (*but avoid*)
allot, allotted, allotting
all ready (set to go), already (beforehand)
all right (*two words; not* alright)
All Saints' Day (Nov. 1)
all-star
    —an all-star team, game
    —The Canadian Press's all-star selections
    —National League All-Stars (team)
allusion (indirect reference), illusion (false
    impression)
Almighty, the
Alouette 1, 2 (satellites)
Alps, *but* alpine skiing
al-Qaida
already (beforehand)
alternate (one after the other), alternative (one or
    the other)
aluminum
alumna, alumnae (*fem.*)

alumnus, alumni

Alzheimer's disease (*but* Alzheimer Society of Canada)

a.m., p.m. (*lowercase*)
—2 p.m., 2:30 a.m. EST, EDT

a mari usque ad mare (from sea to sea)

ambassador, the U.S. ambassador
—Ambassador Michael Wilson (capitalize before a name)

Amber Alert (child-abduction response system)

ambience

Ambrozic, Aloysius (Roman Catholic cardinal and former archbishop of Toronto)

amendment, Fifth Amendment (U.S.)

American Federation of Labor-Congress of Industrial Organizations (AFL-CIO)

American Indian Movement (AIM)

American Telephone and Telegraph Co. (AT&T)

America's Cup (yachting)

amiable (of people), amicable (of things)

amok (*not* amuck)

Ampersand — Use when part of an official name: H&R Block and in expressions such as B&B (bed and breakfast). Write out in other uses: Ian and Sylvia.

Amtrak (*not* Amtrack)

analogous

analysis, analyses

analyze (*not* -se), analyzing

anemia, anemic

anesthesia, anesthetic, anesthetist

aneurysm

Anglican Church of Canada
—Anglican communion
—Anglican Church Women
—High Church, Low Church

Anglo, Anglo-Quebecer, Anglos
anglophone (*lowercase*)
Anik F1, F2 (satellites)
Animals—Capitalize breed names derived from
proper names except where usage has
established the lowercase.
—Holstein-Friesian *but* shorthorn
—Clydesdale *but* palomino
—Newfoundland dog *but* dachshund
—Siamese cat *but* angora
anoint
anomaly, anomalies
anorexia nervosa, anorexic
ante (prefix), antechamber, antedate, antenatal,
anteroom
antenna, antennae (*pl.* for feelers of insect, etc.),
antennas (*pl.* for aerials)
anti- (*prefix*), anti-aircraft, anti-Communist,
antihistamine, anti-intellectual, anti-Semitic,
antitrust, antivirus, antiwar
antivenin (*not* anti-venom)
anybody
anyhow
any more (*as in* "I don't want any more candy")
anymore (any longer)
anyone
anyplace
anything
any time (*two words*)
anyway
AOL Canada Inc.
apartheid
Apartment—Capitalize when used specifically, as
when followed by a number; abbreviate when
used in numbered addresses.
—the Rockingham Apartments

A

—in Apt. 207
—Apt. 207, Midtown Terrace
APEC (Asia-Pacific Economic Cooperation)
apostle, Twelve Apostles
—the Apostle Paul
—Paul the Apostle
appal, appalled, appalling
Appaloosa
apparatus, apparatuses
appeal, appealed, appealing, appealingly
Appeal Court
appellant
appellate division (of Supreme Court)
appendix, appendixes
Apples—Capitalize varieties.
—McIntosh, Golden Delicious, Ida Red
April (*no abbvn.*)
April Fool's Day (April 1)
Aqaba, Gulf of
Aqua-Lung (trademark for an underwater
breathing device)
aquarium, aquariums
Arabian Gulf
— *Use* Persian Gulf
arabic numerals
Arafat, Yasser (PLO, 1929-2004)
Aransas (*not* Arkansas) refuge
arbour
arc, arcing, arced
Arcand, Denys (movies)
Archbishop—Capitalize before a name and when
the full title is used.
—Archbishop John Smith
—Archbishop of York
—the archbishop said ...
archdiocese, Toronto archdiocese

archeological, archeologist, archeology

Arctic—Capitalize when referring to the Arctic region: Arctic Circle, Arctic Ocean, Arctic char, Arctic fox, Arctic plant. Lowercase when it meaning very cold: arctic chill, arctic temperatures.

Arden, Jann (musician)

ardour

Argentine (*not* Argentinian)

argyle socks, sweater

Argyll and Sutherland Highlanders of Canada

Arizona (Ariz.)

Arkansas (Ark.) *but* Aransas refuge (for wildlife)

Armed Forces, the Forces (capped for Canada only)

armful, armfuls

armour

arm's-length *(adj.)*

Army—Capitalize Canadian Army when referring to pre-unification force. For other forces, lowercase army when preceded by the name of the country.
>—Canadian Army until 1968
>—British army
>—British 21st Army
>—a convoy of army vehicles
>—1st Canadian Division
>—3rd Infantry Brigade
>—Royal 22nd Regiment
>—1st Battalion, Royal 22nd
>—B Company

Art—Lowercase art styles, schools, movements, etc., unless the word is derived from a proper noun or can be confused with a common word.
>—art deco, art nouveau
>—baroque

A

—cubism, cubist
—Dada, Dadaism
—Gothic
—impressionism, impressionist
—neoclassical
—Renaissance
—Romanesque
arteriosclerosis
Arthabaska, Que. (Athabasca, Alta.)
arthroscopy
article
—a paragraph of Article 4
—Art. 4, Sec. 1, reads:
artifact
Arviat, Nunavut (formerly Eskimo Point)
Aryan Nations (white supremacist group)
ascend, ascendance, ascendant, ascension, ascent
—Ascension Day
Ashrawi, Hanan (Palestinian)
Ash Wednesday
asinine
Aspirin (trademark in Canada)
Assad, Bashar (Syria)
assassin, assassination
assembly
—National Assembly (national legislative
body)
—Quebec national assembly (provincial
body)
—legislative assembly
assistant (*lowercase*), assistant attorney general Erin
Keenan
assizes, spring assizes
Associated Press, The (for AP)
—and The Associated Press said ...
—the Associated Press story said ...

—the AP (*second reference; lowercase* the)

Association of South East Asian Nations (ASEAN)

Associations—Capitalize names, but follow French style for French names.

> —Société pour vaincre la pollution
> —Association of the Scientific, Engineering and Technological Community of Canada (Scitec)
> —Canadian Bankers Association
> —the association meeting

Astronomy—Capitalize the proper names of planets, stars, constellations; capitalize only the proper-noun element of the name of comets, etc.; lowercase sun and moon. In general, lowercase earth, but capitalize it when referred to as an astronomical body.

> —Saturn, North Star, Orion
> —Halley's comet, Crab nebula
> —down to earth
> —heaven on earth
> —The planets closest to the sun are Mercury, Venus and Earth.
> —The astronauts turned back to Earth.

Astroturf (trademark for artificial grass or turf)

Atamanenko, Alex (MP)

AT&T (*no spaces*), for American Telephone and Telegraph Co.

Athabasca, Alta. (Arthabaska, Que.)

Athapaskan (aboriginal languages)

atherosclerosis (a form of arteriosclerosis with fatty degeneration)

Athlete of the Year

Athletes Can (*not* CAN)

athlete's foot

Atikamekw (First Nations in Quebec)

Atlantic provinces (N.B., N.L., N.S., P.E.I.)

Atomic Energy of Canada Ltd. (AECL *OK in second reference*)

attorney (U.S.; *prefer* lawyer)

attorney, Crown
—Crown attorney Ellen Tomcik
—power of attorney (*no hyphens*)

attorney general, attorneys general
—Attorney General Madalene Phillips

Audit Bureau of Circulations (ABC)

auditor general, auditors general, auditor general Sheila Fraser (*lowercase*)

auger (tool for boring holes)

augur (bode)

Augustyn, Frank (ballet)

aurora borealis (northern lights); aurora australis (southern equivalent)
—Aurora (patrol aircraft)

authority
—St. Lawrence Seaway Authority

authorize

automaker, autoworker (*but* Canadian Auto Workers union)

automated banking machine, ABM (*avoid* ABM machine *as redundant*)

automaton, automatons

auto pact (signed January 1965)

avant-garde

Avenue—Capitalize when used with names; abbreviate in numbered street addresses.
—along Portage Avenue
—the Portage Avenue bus
—506 Curry Ave., Windsor, Ont. N9B 2B9

averse (reluctant), adverse (unfavourable)

avocado, avocados

Avro Arrow (the CF-105 interceptor aircraft built by A.V. Roe Canada Ltd. in the 1950s)

AWACS (for airborne warning and control system)

Awards—Capitalize specific awards.
>   —National Newspaper Awards (NNA)
>   —the awards were presented ...
>   —Governor General's Awards
>   —Nobel Peace Prize
>   —Nobel Prize in chemistry
>   —Nobel Prize winner
>   —Pulitzer Prize
>   —Pulitzer Prize-winning author
>   —Academy Awards

awhile *(adv.), but* a while *(n.)*

AWL (*not* AWOL
>   — absent without leave; *but avoid*)

axe (*not* ax), axing

Axel (figure-skating jump)

axis, axes
>   —Axis, the (Second World War alliance of Germany, Italy and Japan)

Aykroyd, Dan (comic)

Azerbaijan

AZT (HIV-AIDS drug, often called zidovudine)

B

Baath party (Iraq), Baathist (party member)
baby boom, baby boomer, baby boom generation
babysit, babysitter
baccalaureate
Bachand, Claude (politician)
bachelor
      —bachelor of arts (BA), a bachelor's degree
      —bachelor of laws (LLB, *but avoid*)
      —bachelor of science (B.Sc.)
      —honours bachelor degree
bacillus, bacilli
backbench members, backbenchers, backbenches
backbone, back burner, backlog, back roads,
      backstage, backstop (*n.* and *v.*), backup (*n.*
      and *adj.*), backyard.
bacterium, bacteria
Baha'i (*n.* and *adj.*)
      —two Baha'is
      —the Baha'i faith
Bahamas, the
Bahamian (*not* Bahaman)
Bahrain
bail (water or bond)
bail out (of plane)
baked alaska
balaclava
bale (hay)
balk
balkanize
ball, ball club, ball game *but* ballplayer, ballpark
balloon, ballooning, balloonist
ballot, balloting
ballpoint
ballroom, Crystal Ballroom
baloney (slang — nonsense; also informal —
      bologna sausage)

band, the God's River band
Band-Aid (trademark for an adhesive bandage)
B&B (*no spaces*), bed and breakfast
banister (*not* -nn-)
banjo, banjos
Banks—Short forms, rather than corporate names,
      may be used on first reference when their use
      is widespread. *See also separate bank listings.*
      —BMO (Bank of Montreal)
      —CIBC (Canadian Imperial Bank of
      Commerce)
      —HSBC (HSBC Bank Canada)
      —RBC, Royal Bank (Royal Bank of Canada)
      —Scotiabank (Bank of Nova Scotia)
      —TD Bank (Toronto-Dominion Bank)
      —Bank of Canada
      —World Bank
      —the bank's lending policy
baptize (*not* -s-)
bar
      —Canadian Bar Association (CBA, *but avoid*)
      —Bar of the Province of Quebec
      (organization)
      —*but* Quebec bar, Montreal bar, called to the
      bar
Barbados (one island; *do not use* the Barbados)
barbecue (*not* -que), barbecuing
barbiturate
Bardot, Brigitte
barefoot (*no hyphen*)
bar mitzvah (for boy marking 13th birthday), bat
      mitzvah (for girl)
Barnard, Dr. Christiaan (1922-2001)
baroque
Barren Lands, the Barrens
Barrick Gold Inc. (TSX:ABX)

B

Barron's (financial weekly published by Dow
      Jones)

Baryshnikov, Mikhail (ballet)

Baseball—at bat (*but* five at-bats), backstop, ball
      club, ballpark, ballplayer, baseline, bullpen,
      centre field, centre-fielder, centre-field
      fence, change-up, double-A, doubleheader,
      double-play, earned-run average, fastball,
      first baseman, home plate, home run,
      left-fielder, left-hander, line up (*v.*), lineup
      (*n.*), major league (*n.*), major-league (*adj.*),
      a major-leaguer (*n.*), pinch hit (*n.* and *v.*),
      pinch-hitter (*n.*), play off (*v.*), playoff (*n., adj.*),
      RBI(s), put out (*v.*), putout (*n.*), right-fielder,
      right-hander, shortstop, shut out (*v.*), shutout
      (*n., adj.*), single-A, split-finger fastball,
      triple-A, triple-play, twi-night doubleheader

Basel, Switzerland

BASIC (for beginner's all-purpose symbolic
      instruction code)

basis, bases

Basketball—backboard, backcourt, baseline,
      field goal, foul line, foul shot, free throw,
      free-throw line, frontcourt, full-court press,
      goaltending, half-court pass, halftime,
      in-bounds pass, jump ball, jump shot,
      layup, man-to-man (*adj.*), midcourt, play
      off (*v.*), playoff (*n., adj.*), three-point play,
      three-pointer

basset (dog)

battalion, 3rd Battalion

Battle Harbour, N.L.

Battles—Capitalize specific ones.
      —Battle of the Plains of Abraham
      —Battle of Britain

bauxite

bay, Hudson Bay, Bay of Quinte
  —Hudson's Bay Co., the Bay
bazaar
BB (shot)
BC—Acceptable in all references for before Christ.
  It follows the year or the century: 55 BC, the
  second century BC.
BCE Inc. (TSX:BCE)
  —Bell Canada
  —Bell Aliant (TSX:BA.UN)
  —Bell ExpressVu
  —Bell Mobility
  —Sympatico (Internet service)
BC Ferries *(no periods)*
BC Hydro *(no periods)*
beau, beaus
beef Stroganoff
Beethoven, Ludwig van *(not* von) (1770-1827)
behaviour
behoove *(not* behove)
Beijing (formerly Peking)
Belarus (formerly Byelorussia), Belarusian
Belize (formerly British Honduras)
belligerent
bellwether
Belmont Stakes
beluga (whale)
benefit, benefited, benefiting
Benin (Dahomey until 1975)
Bergeron, Stéphane (politician)
Berkeley, Calif.
Berlin Wall
Bermudian *(not* Bermudan)
Bern, Switzerland
berserk
Berton, Pierre (1920-2004)

B

besieged (*not* beseiged)
bestseller (*one word*), bestselling author
bettor (one who wagers)
Beverly Hills, Calif.
Bevilacqua, Maurizio (politician)
BHP Billiton Ltd. (Australia-based mining
    company)
Bible, Bible Belt
    —*but* the fisherman's bible
biblical
Bic (trademark for pen)
bicultural, bilingual (*no hyphen*)
Biennial, bimonthly, biweekly—These terms
    are ambiguous and can mean two different
    things. *Prefer* every two years, twice a month,
    twice a week, etc.
Big Ten (universities)
big-time (*adj.*), big time (*n.*)
bill
    —Bill 101
    —a proposed bill of rights
billet, billeted, billeting
Binghamton, N.Y.
bin Laden, Osama
bioterrorism, bioterrorist
biracial (*no hyphen*)
birdie (one stroke under par in golf)
Birks Jewellers (store)
    —Henry Birks and Sons Inc.
Birney, Earle (poet, 1904-1995)
birth, birthday, birthmark, birthrate, birthright
Bishkek, Kyrgyzstan (formerly Frunze, Kirghizia)
Bishop—Capitalize before a name and when the
    full title is used.
    —Bishop Edward Tremaine
    —Bishop of London

—the bishop's letter

Bismarck (*not* -rk)

bismuth (commodity)

black (*lowercase* for race)

BlackBerry (wireless device), BlackBerrys

blackfly, blackflies

Blackhawks, Chicago

Black Muslim (member of Black Muslims organization; official name: the Nation of Islam)

black out (*v.*), blackout (*n.* and *adj.*)

Black Panther (member of Black Panthers organization)

Blaikie, Bill (politician)

bleached-kraft pulp

blindsided

bloc (of parties, countries; voted as a bloc)
—Bloc Québécois
—former East Bloc

block (of shares, seats; also mental block)

blog, blogger, blogging

blond (*n.* and *adj.* for all uses; do not use blonde)

bloodbath (*one word*)

bloodthirsty (*one word*)

Bloody Mary (nickname for Mary I), bloody mary (cocktail)

blue, Double Blue (Toronto Argonauts)

blue-line (hockey)

Bluenose II (ship)

BMO Financial Group (TSX:BMO)
—BMO Bank of Montreal (Canadian banking operation)

B'nai Brith (Sons of the Covenant)

BNN—Use Business News Network *in first reference* (formerly Report on Business Television)

Board—Uppercase when using the formal name of

a board. Otherwise, lowercase.
—Toronto District School Board, but Toronto school board, public school board
—Board of Trade, the board
—Canadian Wheat Board, the wheat board
—Treasury Board, the board

boat, lifeboat, motorboat, powerboat, sailboat

bobsled, bobsledding
—Bobsleigh Canada

bocce (game)

bodycheck

bodyguard (*no hyphen*)

boe per day (*prefer* barrels of oil equivalent per day)

bogey, bogeys, bogeyed (for one over par)

bohemian (unconventional); Bohemian (of Czech region)

boldface (type)

Bomarc-A, Bomarc-B

bombardier (*no abbvn.*)

Bombardier Inc. (TSX:BBD.B)

Bombay — *Use* Mumbai

bombshell (*one word*)

bona fide (*adj.* — genuine; *adv.* — genuinely), bona fides (*n.* — proof of status)

bonspiel

bonus, bonuses

bookkeeper, bookkeeping

Book of Common Prayer

Book of Revelation (*not* Revelations)

Bophuthatswana (former homeland state in South Africa)

borscht, Borscht Belt

Bosnia-Herzegovina, Bosnia

Botox (trademark)

Bouctouche, N.B.

Boulevard—Capitalize when used with names;

abbreviate in numbered street addresses.
—on Decarie Boulevard
—123 Decarie Blvd.

bound (*suffix*), eastbound, northbound, stormbound

bourbon (American whiskey)

Bourgeoys, St. Marguerite (Canada's first woman saint, 1620-1700)

Boutros-Ghali, Boutros

bovine spongiform encephalopathy (better known as mad cow disease; BSE OK *but explain*)

bowl, Rose Bowl, Super Bowl

bowling
—fivepin, tenpin

boxcar

Boxing—Most weight classes are one word: flyweight, bantamweight, heavyweight.
—knockout

boyfriend, girlfriend

braggadocio

braille

Brantford Expositor

Brasilia (capital of Brazil)

Bravo (*not* Bravo!) TV channel

breach (*n.* — breaking or neglect; *v.* — break through)

break (*v.*), break away, break down, break even, break in, break off, break out, break up

break (*n.*), breakaway, breakdance, breakdown, break-in, breakneck, breakout, breakup, breakthrough, breakwater

breastfeed

breathalyzer

Brébeuf, St. Jean de (1593-1649)

breech (back part of gun barrel), breeches (short trousers), breeches-buoy

Breitkreuz, Garry (politician)

B

Bren gun
Bre-X Minerals Ltd. (defunct)
Brezhnev, Leonid (1906-1982)
bridge, Lions Gate Bridge, Sydney Harbour Bridge
Brier (curling tournament), Tim Hortons Brier
brigadier (Brig. Arthur Smith)
brigadier-general (Brig.-Gen. Arthur Smith)
Brink's Canada Ltd.
>—*but* a Brinks truck, Brinks guard (*no apostrophe*)

Britain—The one island: England, Scotland, Wales. (*But* British also covers Northern Ireland.)
Britannia
British Airways (*no abbvn.*)
British Columbia (B.C.)
British Commonwealth (*prefer* the Commonwealth)
British North America Act (BNA Act)
British thermal unit(s), BTU(s)
Briton (*not* Britisher)
broach (open; begin to talk about)
broccoli
Brockville Recorder and Times
Bromo Seltzer (trademark for bicarbonate of soda)
brooch (ornament)
Bros. for company names *but* Brothers with entertainment groups: the Mills Brothers
brouhaha
Brueggergosman, Measha (singer)
Bruinooge, Rod (MP)
brussels sprouts
Brzezinski, Zbigniew
Buckingham Palace
Buddha, Buddhism, Buddhist
budget, budgetary, budgeted, budgeting
buffalo, buffaloes
Building—Capitalize important buildings.

    —Parliament Buildings
    —Empire State Building
    —Aetna Life building
build up (*v.*), buildup (*n., adj.*), built-up (*adj*)
Bujold, Geneviève (actor)
bulimia
bullmastiff *(one word)*
Bullock, Sandra (actor)
bull's-eye
bumf (papers, documents)
bungee jumping
Bunyan, Paul
buoy, buoyant, buoyancy
bureau, bureaus
burka
Burkina Faso (formerly Upper Volta)
Burk's Falls, Ont.
Burton, Richard (actor, 1925-1984)
bus (vehicle), buses, busing
Busan, South Korea (*not* Pusan)
Bush, George W. (use initial to distinguish from
    father, George Bush)
businessman, businesswoman
Business News Network (formerly Report on
    Business Television; BNN *on second reference*)
buss (kiss), busses
Buthelezi, Mangosuthu (Zulu leader)
buttonhole (*no hyphen*)
byelection (*no hyphen*)
bylaw (*no hyphen*)
byline (*no hyphen*)
bypass (*no hyphen*)
byproduct (*no hyphen*)
byte (unit of computer memory)

C

C (use for Canadian currency: C$500)
cabinet, cabinet council
cable TV (*no hyphen*)
cacophony
cactus, cacti
cadet
>   —officer cadet (*no abbvn.*)
>   —Officer Cadet Garth Atkins
Cadillac
CAE Inc. (TSX:CAE)
Caesar, Julius (c. 102-44 BC)
caesarean birth, section (*lowercase*), *but* C-section
caesar salad
Caesars Palace (Las Vegas — *no apostrophe*)
café
caffeine
Cage, Nicolas (actor)
caisse populaire (credit union), caisses populaires
Calder Memorial Trophy (NHL's top rookie)
calibre, a .45-calibre pistol
California (Calif.)
Callaghan, Morley (novelist, 1903-1990)
Callbeck, Catherine (senator)
callisthenics
callous (*adj.* — unfeeling), callus (*n.* — thickened skin)
call-up (*n.*)
calorie
camaraderie
Cambodia (Kampuchea 1975-90)
Canada
>   —Central Canada (Ontario and Quebec)
>   —Eastern Canada (the Atlantic provinces,
>   Quebec and Ontario)
>   —Lower Canada (present-day Quebec)
>   —Upper Canada (present-day Ontario)
>   —Western Canada (Manitoba, Saskatchewan,

Alberta and British Columbia)

Canada AM (CTV show)

Canada Council for the Arts, Canada Council, the
council

Canada Cup (hockey)

Canada Customs, customs
—go through customs, a customs officer

Canada Day (July 1)

Canada Industrial Relations Board (CIRB, *but avoid*)

Canada Mortgage and Housing Corp. (CMHC)

Canada NewsWire (CNW in second reference)

Canada Pension Plan (CPP, *but avoid*)

Canada Revenue Agency (formerly Canada
Customs and Revenue Agency)

Canadarm 2

Canada Savings Bond (CSB)

Canada's Cup (yachting)

Canada West Foundation

Canada-wide (*adj.*)

Canadian Alliance (now Conservative Party of
Canada)

Canadian Association of Broadcasters (CAB)

Canadian Auto Workers (CAW *in second reference*)

Canadian Bankers Association

Canadian Blood Services

Canadian Coast Guard
—the coast guard ship
—coastguardman (*one word*)

Canadian Community Newspapers Association

Canadian Conference of Catholic Bishops (*not*
Council)

Canadian Food Inspection Agency

Canadian Forces, the Forces (*capped for Canadian
only*)
—Canadian Forces Headquarters (CFHQ, *but
avoid*)

—a Canadian Forces base
—Canadian Forces Base Trenton, CFB Trenton
(second reference)
—CFB TRENTON (placeline)
Canadian government
Canadian Heritage (for Department of Canadian
Heritage; *do not use* Heritage Canada, which is
an unrelated organization)
Canadian Institutes of Health Research (formerly
Medical Research Council of Canada)
Canadian Interuniversity Sport (CIS *in second
reference*)
Canadian Journalism Fellowships (formerly
Southam Fellowships)
—Canadian Journalism Fellow
Canadian Manufacturers & Exporters (formerly
Alliance of Manufacturers & Exporters
Canada)
Canadian National, or CN
—Canadian National Railway Co. (formal
name; TSX:CNR)
—CN Tower
Canadian National Institute for the Blind — *Use*
CNIB
Canadian Newspaper Association (CNA, *but avoid*)
Canadian Nuclear Safety Commission (formerly
Atomic Energy Control Board)
Canadian Opera Company (*not* Co.)
Canadian Pacific Railway Ltd. (TSX:CP)
—CPR on second reference
Canadian Paediatric Society
Canadian Press, The
Canadian Professional Golfers' Association (CPGA)
Canadian Radio-television and
Telecommunications Commission (CRTC *OK*
in first reference)

Canadian Security Intelligence Service (CSIS)
Canadian Shield
Canadian Space Agency
Canadian Taxpayers Federation
Canadian Tire Corp. Ltd. (TSX:CTC.A)
Canadian Transportation Agency
Canadian Wheat Board (*no abbvn.*)
Canadian Wildlife Service (*no abbvn.*)
canal, Panama Canal, Suez Canal, Welland Canal
    —Panama Canal Zone (district)
cancel, cancelled, cancelling
Cancer, Tropic of
Cancon (*OK in second reference* for Canadian
    content)
candour
Candu (for Canadian deuterium uranium reactor)
Canfor Corp. (TSX:CFP)
canister
canoeist
cantaloupe
canto, cantos
Canuck
canvas, canvases (cloth, painting)
canvass (*v.* — examine; seek votes, orders; *n.* —
    process of canvassing)
Canwest Global Communications Corp. (TSX:CGS)
    —Canwest News Service
canyon, Grand Canyon
Cap-aux-Meules, Que.
Cape Breton (*never in placeline*)
Cape Town (*two words*)
Capitol (building at Washington, D.C.) *but* state
    capitol (*lowercase*)
cappuccino, cappuccinos
captain, Capt. (*but* team captain Joan Verona)
Cara Operations Ltd.

C

carat (gems), karat (gold), caret (printing)
carburetor
cardinal (*no abbvn.*)
> —John Cardinal Smith
> —the cardinal (or Smith) said ...

CARE (for Co-operative for American Relief
> Everywhere Inc.)

caregiver
cargo, cargoes
Caribbean Community (federation)
Caribbean Free Trade Area (Carifta, *but avoid*)
Cariboo Mountains (B.C.)
caribou (deer), Caribou (Inuit, plane)
Caribou Mountains (Alta.)
carillon, carillonneur
carjack, carjacking (*v.* and *n.*)
Carleton, N.S. and Que.
> —Carleton Place, Ont.
> —Carleton University (Ottawa)
> —Carleton Village, N.S.
> —*but* Carlton, Sask.
> —Carlton Street (Toronto)
> —Ritz-Carlton Hotel

carmaker
carpet, carpet-bag, carpet-sweeper
Cartier, George-Etienne (1814-1873)
cartilage
cassette, videocassette
catalogue (*not* catalog)
catch-22 (a dilemma from which there is no escape);
> *Catch-22* (Joseph Heller's book)

category, Category 2
Caterpillar, a Cat (trademark for a tractor)
Catholic, Catholicism (*but* specify Roman Catholic
> or Roman Catholicism *on first reference* if
> reference excludes Eastern-rites Catholic

churches.
catholic (universal)
CAT scan — *Use* CT scan
Cattle—Capitalize breed names derived from
proper names except where usage has
established the lowercase.
—Holstein-Friesian
—Jersey, Guernsey, Ayrshire
—shorthorn
Caucasian
cave in (*v.*), cave-in (*n.*)
CBC (*acceptable in all references* for Canadian
Broadcasting Corp.)
—CBC-TV, CBC Radio One, CBC Radio Two
—*The Current, The National, Newsworld*
CBS Inc.
—CBS's coverage
CD-ROM (compact disc read-only memory);
acceptable in all references
cease fire (*v.*), ceasefire (*n.*)
Ceausescu, Nicolae (Romanian leader, 1918-1989)
Celanese (trademark for acetate, nylon, polyester,
rayon)
Celestica Inc. (TSX:CLS)
cellblock (in jail)
cellophane, celluloid, cellulose
cellphone (cellular phone)
Celsius, -30 C (hyphen, no period; specify Celsius
only to avoid confusion)
cement (powder; used in concrete)
cemetery, Ocean View Cemetery
census, censuses, census day
Centennial Year, the Centennial (1967)
—*but* Canada's centennial
—centennial celebrations
Centers for Disease Control and Prevention

C

(Atlanta, full name; Centers for Disease
Control *OK in first reference*)
—*Use* U.S. Centers for Disease Control *if
necessary* to make clear it is American centre
centimetre (cm — *sing.* and *pl.* metric symbol, no
period)
Central Canada (Ontario and Quebec)
Central Committee
Centrale de l'enseignement du Québec (Quebec
teachers federation)
centre, centred, centring
—centre on (*not* around)
—centre field (baseball)
—centre-fielder
—centre-field wall
—John F. Kennedy Center for the Performing
Arts
—Air Canada Centre
—Rockefeller Center
Centre of Forensic Sciences (Toronto)
centurion (Roman soldier), Centurion (tank)
century, 20th century, second-century Rome
CEO (*OK in first reference* for chief executive officer)
CFCs (chlorofluorocarbons)
CF-18 (Canadian designation for the McDonnell
Douglas aircraft)
chamber, lower chamber
—Chamber of Deputies
—Halifax Chamber of Commerce
—the chamber of commerce
changeover (*n.*), change over (*v.*)
channel
—Channel 10 (television)
—English Channel and the Channel
—Channel Tunnel (between Britain and
France)

C

chaperon (*not* -one)

Chappaquiddick Island, Mass.

chapter (*no abbvn.*), Chapter 1

chargé(s) d'affaires, chargé d'affaires John O'Hara

chargeback (*n.* and *adj.*)

charley horse

Charlottetown accord

Charter of Rights and Freedoms, the charter, charter rights

chat room

check (restaurant bill)

checkerboard, checkers, checkered flag (motor racing), checkered career

check off (*v.*), checkoff (*n.*)

checkpoint (*one word*), Checkpoint Charlie

check up (*v.*), checkup (*n.*)

Chedabucto Bay, N.S.

cheddar cheese

chef-d'oeuvre, chefs-d'oeuvre

Chekhov, Anton (Russian writer, 1860-1904)

Chemical elements—Write out *in first reference* (carbon dioxide) but symbols *OK in second reference* if popularly used: CO2.

Chennai, India (formerly Madras)

cheque (bank), chequebook

Chernomyrdin, Viktor (Russian politician)

cherub, cherubs

Chiang Kai-shek (1887-1975)

Chianti (wine)

chickenpox

chief

  —Chief Tom Whitefeather

  —police Chief Anna Myers

  —fire Chief Ron Espy

chief master sergeant

  —Chief Master Sgt. Phil McDonald

C

chief petty officer (*no abbvn.*)
chief warrant officer (*no abbvn.*)
childish (silly, puerile), childlike (innocent, trusting)
Children's Aid Society
Chile
chili, chilies
    —chili con carne
    —chili sauce
China, People's Republic of (mainland, *but prefer simply* China)
china (crockery)
Chinese (*n* and *adj.*)
Chinese Names—Use the official Chinese spelling, Pinyin, for most personal and place names: Hua Guofeng (formerly Hua Kuofeng). Note that the family name (Hua) normally precedes the given name (Guofeng). But westernized Chinese often follow English practice: Robert Chow (*not* Chow Robert).
   Use the traditional spellings for Shanghai and Tibet. But use Zhou Enlai (*not* Chou En lai) and Mao Zedong (*not* Mao Tse-tung).
chinook
Chipewyan (aboriginal band)
chipmaker (*one word*)
chisel, chiselled, chiseller
chlorophyll
choose, chose, chosen, choosing, choosy
Chornobyl (Ukraine)
Choyce, Lesley (writer)
Chrétien, Jean
Christie's (auctioneer)
Christmas Day, Eve
chromosome
Church—Capitalize in names of religions and buildings.

—Roman Catholic Church, Catholic Church,
Anglican Church; *but* the church (*lowercase*)
—St. Bartholomew's Church (building), the
church (building)
—a church building, church doctrine
Church of Christ, Scientist (Christian Science
Church *OK in first reference*)
Church of Jesus Christ of Latter-day Saints
(Mormons)
chute (sluice, slide, parachute)
chutzpah (gall, audacity)
CIBC (TSX:CM)
—CIBC (for Canadian Imperial Bank of
Commerce) *OK in first reference*
—CIBC World Markets Inc. (corporate and
investment banking arm); CIBC Wood Gundy
(retail investment division)
cigarette
cipher (*not* cypher)
circle (Circ.)
Circle, Arctic
—*but* arctic winds, temperatures
Cirque du soleil
cirrhosis
citizens band (CB, *but avoid*)
—citizens-band radio (*hyphen*)
city, city council
—Halifax City Hall (proper name)
—city hall (administration, building)
—City of Halifax (corp.)
—*but* in the city of Halifax
—Quebec City (Quebec in placelines)
Citytv (Toronto)
—CityPulse
—CablePulse 24
Civil Aeronautics Board (U.S.)

C

Civil Service Commission (*no abbvn.*)
civil war
> —Spanish Civil War
> —Civil War (U.S.)

clamour
clangour (*but* clangorous)
Claridge's (London hotel)
Clark, Joe (former prime minister)
Clarke, Austin (novelist)
Clarkson, Adrienne
Class—Lowercase school classes, except languages.
> —class of '61
> —mathematics class
> —French class

class (military)
> —S-class submarine
> —tribal-class destroyer

class A, class B (shares)
clean up (*v.*), cleanup (*n.*)
clear cut (*v.*), clearcut (*n.*)
cliché
clientele
climactic (of a climax), climatic (of climate)
cloverleaf (on highways), cloverleafs
Club—Capitalize names.
> —Rotary Club
> —a club officer

CNIB (formerly Canadian National Institute for the Blind)
CN Tower (Toronto)
co- (prefix), coadjutor, co-author (*n. only*), coaxial, co-chairman, coexist, co-host, co-operate, co-ordinate, co-owner, co-pilot (*n. only*), co-worker.
coast
> —East Coast, West Coast, Gulf Coast

(regions), B.C. coast, Atlantic coast
(shorelines)
coast guard
—Canadian Coast Guard
—U.S. Coast Guard
—the coast guard, the coast guard ship
coastline *(one word)*
cobalt-60
Cobol (common business oriented language)
Cobourg, Ont.
Coca-Cola, Coke (trademarks for cola drink)
coccus, cocci
cockney
Codco (comedy TV)
code, city building code
—Criminal Code, the code
—Morse code
coed (*avoid* as a noun for female student. *OK* as an
adjective meaning coeducational: coed dorm)
Cogeco Cable Inc. (TSX:CCA)
cognoscente (*sing.*), cognoscenti (*pl.*)
coho (salmon — *sing.* and *pl.*)
Coke (as trade name for Coca-Cola)
Cold War
Colisée (Quebec City arena)
collectible(s)
College—Capitalize the names of universities and
colleges.
—McGill University
—University of Toronto (U of T)
—Victoria College
College of Cardinals
collegiate, York Collegiate (capitalize when part of
official name)
Collins Bay, Ont.
—Collins Bay Penitentiary

Colombia (South America)
Colombo Plan
colonel (Col. Eric Anderson)
Colorado (Colo.)
Colosseum (Rome)
colour, colourize, colourist *but* colorific
Colville, Alex (painter)
Comaneci, Nadia (former gymnast)
combat, combated, combatant
come back (*v.*), comeback (*n.*)
Come By Chance, N.L.
command, Maritime Command
commander (Cmdr. Wayne Elder)
 —lieutenant-commander (Lt.-Cmdr.)
 —wing commander (Wing Cmdr.)
commander-in-chief
commander of the Order of the British Empire
 (CBE)
commandment
 —the Ten Commandments
 —the Tenth Commandment
commando, commandos
command sergeant major
 —Command Sgt. Maj. Claude Laporte
commensurate
commiserate
Commission—Capitalize the proper name of
 government and royal commissions.
 —Commission on the Future of Health Care
 but the health-care commission
commitment
committal
committee
 —Commons finance committee
commodore (*no abbvn.*)
Common Prayer, Book of

Commons, House of
>—the House, the Commons

common sense, a common-sense approach

commonwealth
>—the Commonwealth
>—Commonwealth of Australia
>—Commonwealth Development Bank
>—Commonwealth Games, the Games
>—Co-operative Commonwealth Federation (CCF)

communion, holy communion
>—Anglican communion

communism (philosophical attitude)

Communist (party, government or member)
>—anti-communist, non-communist, pro-communist

communist ideals (philosophical)

Companies' Creditors Arrangement Act (CCAA *OK in second reference*)

Company—Use Co. in business names.
>—American Broadcasting Cos. (ABC)
>—Brown Co.
>—*but* Canadian Opera Company (entertainment)
>—B Company (military)

company quartermaster-sergeant (*no abbvn.*)

company sergeant major (Company Sgt. Maj. John Jones)
>—company sergeants major

compare to (liken to), compare with (check similarities and differences)

compatible

compel, compelled, compelling

competent (*not* -ant)

complementary (serving to complete), complimentary (expressing compliment; free)

C

concede
concept, conception
—Immaculate Conception
concertgoer
concerto, concertos
Concorde (aircraft)
condole, condolence (*not* -ance)
Confederation (Canada)
—Fathers of Confederation
Confederation of National Trade Unions (CNTU);
in French, Confédération des syndicats
nationaux (CSN)
conference
—federal-provincial conference
—Duke of Edinburgh's Study Conference
—Law of the Sea conference
—Conference Board of Canada
confidant (man), confidante (woman)
Confucian
Congo (formerly Zaire, formal name Democratic
Republic of Congo)
Congo, Republic of (capital Brazzaville)
congregation
—Congregation for the Doctrine of the Faith
(Vatican)
Congress (U.S.)
—*but* congressman, congressional
—Sen. John Smith
—Rep. Mary Smith
—Congress party (India)
Congress of Racial Equality (CORE)
Connecticut (Conn.)
connoisseur (-nn-)
Connors, Stompin' Tom (singer-composer)
Conn Smythe Trophy (hockey)
conscientious

consensus (*not* consensus of opinion)

Conservative (party), conservative (political outlook)

    —Conservative Party of Canada (formal name)

    —small-c conservative

constable (Const.)

    —Const. Maria Huang

    —a city constable

constitution, the French Constitution, the constitution; *but* the Constitution (capped in all references to Canada)

consulate, French Consulate, the consulate

consul general, Consul General Guy Tremblay

consumer price index (CPI, *but avoid*)

Consumers' Association of Canada

consummate

contact (*v.*, *adj.* and *n.*)

Contadora (island near Panama)

Continent, the (Europe)

continental shelf

contralto, contraltos

controller (*no abbvn.*)

    —Controller Gillian Towers

convener (*not* -or)

converter (*not* -or)

cookbook

Cools, Anne (senator)

Coon Come, Matthew (Coon Come *in second reference*)

co-operate, co-operation

Co-operative Commonwealth Federation (CCF)

co-ordinate

copy editing, copy editor

copyright

    —Copyright, The Canadian Press

C

CORE (for Congress of Racial Equality)
co-respondent (divorce), correspondent (writer)
cornea (*sing.*), corneas (*pl.*)
Corner Brook, N.L.
Corner Brook Western Star
cornerstone, lay
Cornwall Standard-Freeholder
coronavirus (*one word*)
corporal (Cpl. Jane Smith)
 —lance-corporal (Lance-Cpl.)
Corporation—Use Corp. in business names.
 —Eastman Kodak Corp.
 —British Broadcasting Corp. (BBC)
 —Canadian Broadcasting Corp. (*but* CBC
 preferred)
 —Ontario Lottery and Gaming Corp.
corral, corralled
Correctional Service Canada, correctional service
cosy (*not* cozy)
CO2 (OK *in second reference* for carbon dioxide)
council, city or county council, Peel regional council
 but Canada Council, Quebec Forest Industry
 Council, Council of Atlantic Premiers
councillor (Coun.)
 —Coun. Robert Jones
 —a city councillor
Council of Yukon First Nations
counsel, Crown counsel, Queen's counsel (QC, *but*
 avoid)
counsellor
counterattack, counter-intelligence,
 counter-proposal, counterterrorism
countrywide
County—Capitalize when preceding or following a
 specific term.
 —Huron County

—County Derry

—*but* in the county of Huron

coureur de bois, coureurs de bois

Court—Capitalize superior courts but not lower courts.

 —Admiralty Court

 —Appeal Court

 —Court of Queen's Bench

 —European Court of Justice

 —family court

 —Federal Court, Federal Appeal Court

 —judicial committee of the Privy Council

 —Ontario court of justice (lower court)

 —provincial court

 —small claims court

 —Superior Court (Que.)

 —Superior Court of Justice (Ontario)

 —Supreme Court (fed., prov., state)

 —Tax Court (Canada, U.S.)

 —territorial court (N.W.T.)

 —U.S. Court of Appeals

 —U.S. Court of Military Appeals

 —youth court

 —the court ordered

Courtenay, B.C.

courthouse, courtroom

court martial, courts martial (*n.*), court-martial (*v.*)

Court of St. James's

CourtTV Canada (specialty channel)

Covent Garden (*not* Gardens)

cover up (*v.*), coverup (*n.*)

crackpipe

craftman (*no abbvn.*)

 —Craftman Elwood Greene (military)

 —*but* craftsman (artisan)

Craigellachie, B.C. (where Last Spike was driven in

railway in 1885)
Craigslist
creditor (one owed a debt; *not* -er)
Cree (*sing.* and *pl.*)
crescent (Cres.)
Crête, Paul (politician)
Creutzfeldt-Jakob disease (human spongiform
　　　encephalopathy; CJD OK *but explain*)
　　　　　—variant Creutzfeldt-Jakob disease (variant
　　　　　CJD; the form related to mad cow disease)
crewman, crewwoman, crew member
cricket
　　　　　—England-Australia Test match
　　　　　—the Test
　　　　　—the Ashes
Crime Stoppers (*two words*)
Criminal Code, the code
crisis, crises
criterion, criteria
criticism, criticize (*not* -ise)
Croat(s) (*n.*), Croatian (*adj.*)
CROP Inc. (Centre de recherches sur l'opinion
　　　publique; Quebec-based polling firm)
Crosby, Sidney (hockey)
cross-border
cross-checking
cross-country
cross-examine, cross-examination
crossfire
crossover (vehicle, music)
Crow, Sheryl (singer)
crown
　　　　　—the Crown (judge or prosecutor)
　　　　　—the Crown alleges ...
　　　　　—Crown attorney, counsel
　　　　　—Crown attorney Liz Baker

—a Crown corporation, Crown land
—a crown prince
—*but* Crown Prince Rupert
Crowsnest Pass
Crucifixion
cruise (missile)
Crusades
crybaby (*no hyphen*), crybabies
CSeries jet (Bombardier)
CT scan (computerized tomography)
CTVglobemedia
CTV Newsnet
cubism, cubist
Cultural Revolution (China)
cummings, e.e. (1894-1962)
cup, Stanley Cup (trophy)
—America's Cup (yachting)
—Canada Cup (hockey)
—Canada's Cup (yachting)
cupful, cupfuls
Curia (Vatican office)
Curling—bonspiel, free-guard zone, hog line,
in-turn draw, out-turn draw, shot rock
curriculum, curricula
curtain, Iron Curtain
curtsy, curtsies
CUSO (OK *in first reference*, originally stood for
Canadian University Service Overseas)
customs, Canada Customs
—a customs officer
—go through customs
CUV (crossover utility vehicle)
CVRD Inco (mining company formed after
Companhia Vale do Rio Doce of Brazil bought
Inco in 2006)
cyberspace

C

cyclosporine
cystic fibrosis
czar, Czar Nicholas
Czech Republic

D

dachshund

Dacotah, Man.

Dacron (trademark for polyester fibre)

Dahomey (Benin since 1975)

DaimlerChrysler

Dalai Lama, the

Dalmatian

dame, Dame Maggie Smith (*but avoid*), Smith (*second reference*)

damn, damned, damn it, God damn

Dances—Lowercase names.
>—break dancing, bump, charleston, foxtrot, go-go, minuet, pas de deux, polka, polonaise, twist

danish (pastry)

Dar es Salaam
>—DAR ES SALAAM (in placelines)

Dari (language dominant in Afghanistan)

Dark Ages

Dash 8

data (*plural* in scientific writing but usually *singular* in other uses)

databank, database

dateline, placeline
>—*but* international date line

Dates—Write December 2004 without commas and Dec. 14, 2004, with commas. In dates, abbreviate the months except March, April, May, June and July: Aug. 1, May 3. Write Christmas 2005.
>—1997-98 but 1999-2002

Day—Capitalize religious holidays and feasts and all special times.
>—All Saints' Day
>—Christmas Eve
>—Earth Day

D

—*but* election day

daycare (*n.*), daycare centre *(adj.)*

daylight (*not* daylight saving) time
> Applies from second Sunday in March until first Sunday in November except in regions that exempt themselves
> —ADT, EDT, etc.

daylong (*one word*)

day trader

D-Day (June 6, 1944)

DDT (dichlorodiphenyltrichloroethane)

de- (*prefix*), deactivate, debar, decompress,
> de-emphasize, de-escalate, defrost, de-ice, de-ink, deodorize, destabilize

de, der, di, du, d'—When lowercase in names, capitalize only at start of sentence.
> —de Gaulle, Charles
> —de Havilland Inc. (division of Bombardier Inc.)
> —De Laurentiis, Dino (movies)
> —deMille, Cecil B. (movies)
> —deWit, Willie (boxing)
> —de facto (two words — existing, whether legal or not)
> —de jure (two words — by right, by law; *but avoid*)
> —deluxe (*one word)*
> —de rigueur (*not* -geur)

dean, dean of arts

debacle

debonair

deceive, deceivable (*not* -eable), deceiver

decision-making

-decker, double-decker

Decorations—Capitalize specific names.
> —Distinguished Service Cross (DSC)

64

decrepit

deductible (*not* -able)

deejay — *Use* DJ

deepsea (*adj., no hyphen*)

Deep South (U.S.)

defence (*not* defense), *but* defensive

defenceman (*one word*)

defuse (remove fuse), diffuse (spread)

Dehcho First Nation

Deja View (specialty TV channel)

Delaware (Del.)

delicatessen

delta, Mekong River Delta

demagogue, demagogy (*not* -goguery)

demeanour

Democrat

Democratic party (U.S.)

    —New Democratic Party (NDP)

    —a New Democrat

Dene (pronounced Den'-neh)

    —Dene Nation (represents aboriginals in Northwest Territories)

Denendeh (Dene name for Northwest Territories)

Deng Xiaoping, Deng (1904-1997)

Denim Pine (trademark for wood stained blue by activities of mountain pine beetles)

Departments—Capitalize international, national and provincial government departments and ministries. Lowercase municipal, school and business departments.

    —Department of National Defence

    —Defence Department

    —Department of Indian and Northern Affairs

    —Indian Affairs Department

    —Vietnam Health Ministry

Lowercase department in plural uses.

—the Defence and Industry departments
Capitalize the proper-name element when
standing alone and used as noun meaning the
department.

—She went to Defence from Industry.

—*but* Toronto parks department

—McGill history department

It is not necessary to use the full formal name
of a department if a shorter version is clear:
Fisheries Department, *not* Department of
Fisheries and Oceans or Fisheries and Oceans
Canada.

dependant (*n.*), dependent (*adj.*),
    dependence (*not* -ance)

deprecate (disapprove), depreciate (belittle, lose
    value)

Depression (or Great Depression), the (1930s)

deputy

—Deputy Prime Minister Linda Graves,
Deputy Chief Joe Jones (formal title)

—deputy premier Saul Hillier (informal
position)

—deputy Speaker Jean Turcotte

—the deputy Speaker

—deputy Crown attorney Alys Yamata

de rigueur (*not* riguer)

descendant (offspring)

descendent (descending)

-designate, prime minister-designate John Block,
    the chairman-designate

desirable (*not* -eable)

desktop (*one word*)

desperate, desperation

despoliation (*not* despoilation)

detective

—Det. Fred Lisak (police)

—private detective James Brown
deterrent (*not* -ant)
Detroit Three (GM, Ford, Chrysler; *preferred to* Big
    Three except in historical references)
Deutsche Grammophon (recordings)
Deutschmark (*prefer* German mark)
Devoir, Le (Montreal newspaper)
devotee
DEW (for Distant Early Warning) Line
Dhaka, Bangladesh
Dhalla, Ruby (politician)
diabetes, Type 1, Type 2 diabetes
dialed, dialing
dial up *(v.)*, dial-up *(adj., n.)*
dialysis
diameter
Diana, or Princess of Wales (*not* Princess Diana)
diaphragm
diarrhea
Diavik (diamond mine in Northwest Territories)
DiCaprio, Leonardo (actor)
Dickensian
Dictaphone (trademark for a dictation recorder)
die, dying
Diefenbaker, John (1895-1979)
diehard
Diet (national legislative body)
dietitian
diffuse (spread), defuse (remove fuse)
Dijon mustard
dike (barrier; *not* dyke)
dilemma
dilettante, dilettantes
DiMaggio, Joe (1914-1999)
dining room
diocese, Hamilton diocese

D

Dion, Stéphane
diphtheria
diphthong
disaster, disastrous
disc, compact disc (CD, CD-ROM), slipped disc,
    disc brake, disc jockey *but* floppy disk,
    diskette
discernible (*not* -able)
discolour *but* discoloration
Discovery Channel, the (TV)
discreet (circumspect), discrete (separate, abstract)
disease, legionnaires' disease, Minamata disease
dishonour
disingenuous (insincere)
disinterested (impartial), uninterested (not
    interested)
dispel, dispelled
dissension (*not* -tion)
dissociate (*not* disassociate)
distil, distiller
Distinguished Service Cross (DSC)
district attorney, district attorney Mike Fuhrmann
Ditto (trademark for copier)
dived (*not* dove)
divisibility, divisible, divisive
division, 6th Division
DJ (*not* deejay), DJs, DJing, DJed
DNA (deoxyribonucleic acid)
Dobson, Fefe (singer)
doctor (Dr., *but avoid* unless health-care
    professional)
    —doctor of laws (LLD)
    —doctor of medicine (MD)
    —doctor of philosophy (PhD)
docudrama
Dofasco Inc. (formerly Dominion Foundries and

Steel Corp.)

dogcatcher, dogfight, doghouse, dog-tag

Dogs—Capitalize breed names derived from
  proper names except where usage has
  established the lowercase.
  —Dalmatian
  —Doberman pinscher
  —German shepherd
  —Newfoundland, Great Dane
  —St. Bernard, Irish terrier
  —*but* alsatian, dachshund, collie, pekinese,
  spaniel, etc.

Dominica (small Caribbean island republic)

Dominican Republic (neighbour of Haiti)

dominion
  —Dominion of Canada

domino, dominoes

Domtar Corp. (TSX:UFS)

donegal tweed
  —*but* County Donegal

Donnybrook (town), donnybrook (riot)

do-not-call list (for telemarketers)

donut—*Use* doughnut

dos and don'ts

Dosanjh, Ujjal (politician)

Dostoyevsky, Fyodor (novelist, 1821-1881)

dot-com (company, millionaire, etc.)

double-A-plus, double-A-minus (bonds)

doublecross, doublecrosser

double-decker

doubleheader (*one word*)

doubletalk

doughnut (*never* donut except in corporate names)

Doukhobor

Dow Jones (*no hyphen*)
  —Dow Jones Canada

—Dow Jones industrial average, Dow Jones industrials

Down East

downhill

down payment (*two words*)

Down syndrome

    —Down Syndrome Association of Canada

Downtown Eastside (Vancouver)

Down Under (Australia and New Zealand)

Doyle, Damhnait (singer)

D'Oyly Carte

draconian

draegerman (mine-rescue worker)

draft (air, money, plan, military, beer)

draftsman

Dragon (sailboat)

Dramamine (trademark for travel-sickness medicine)

dreck

dressing room (*two words*)

drive (Dr.)

    —111 Sutherland Dr.

    —*but* 24 Sussex Drive (official residence)

drive in (*v.*), drive-in (*n.*), drive-thru (*n.*)

driver's licence

Droit, Le (Ottawa-Gatineau newspaper)

drop-down (*adj.*), drop-down menu

drop out (*v.*), dropout (*n.*)

drugstore (*one word*)

dry, drier, driest

    —*but* hair, laundry dryer

Dubai

duchess

    —Duchess of Cornwall (formerly Camilla Parker Bowles)

Duesseldorf, Germany

D

duffel bag, coat
duke, Duke of Windsor
dumbfound
Dunkirk (*not* Dunkerque)
Dunlap, David Dunlap Observatory (near Toronto)
durum wheat
Dutoit, Charles (conductor)
DVD (for digital video disc, *OK in first reference*)
DVR (digital video recorder, *OK in second reference*)
dwarf, dwarfs
dye, dyeing
dynamo, dynamos
dysentery
dysfunction
dyslexia

E

earl, Earl Spencer
　　—Earl of Athlone
Earth—Capitalize when referred to as a planet.
　　—The planets nearest the sun are Mercury,
　　Venus and Earth.
　　—The astronauts turned back to Earth.
　　—down to earth
　　—the good earth
　　—heaven on earth
East—Capitalize regions *but not* their derivatives.
　　Lowercase mere direction or position.
　　—the East (region)
　　—an easterner
　　—Eastern Canada
　　—an eastern Canadian
　　—eastern Canadian markets
　　—The snow moved east over Eastern Canada.
　　—in eastern Quebec
　　—East Coast (region)
　　—east coast (shoreline)
　　—where East meets West
　　—eastern nations
　　—eastern Europe (no longer a bloc)
　　—Eastern Hemisphere
　　—the Far East
East Block (Ottawa)
Eastern Townships (Quebec)
East India, East Indian — *Use* South Asia, South
　　Asian
Eaton's (T. Eaton Co. Ltd., now defunct)
eBay (Capitalize lowercase names at the beginning
　　of a sentence: EBay)
Ebola virus
echo, echoes
E. coli (bacteria)
e-commerce

ecstasy (*lowercase*) (*OK in first reference* for methyl-
enedioxymethamphetamine)

ecumenical council

eczema

Edmonton Road Runners (AHL)

Edmundston, N.B.

EDT (*not* EDST), eastern time

educator (*prefer* teacher)

effect (*n.* — result); (*v.* — bring about)

effrontery (shameless insolence), affront (deliberate
insult)

e.g. (exempli gratia; *avoid*)

Eglin (*not* Elgin) Field, Fla.

Egoyan, Atom (film director)

E.I. du Pont Canada Co.

    —DuPont (U.S.)

    —Samuel F. Du Pont (his usage)

Eiffel Tower (Paris)

Eilat (Israeli port)

Einstein, Albert (1879-1955)

Ekati (diamond mine in Northwest Territories)

El ("the")—ln Arabic names of individuals, the
articles el and al may be used or dropped
depending on the person's preference or
established usage: Osama el-Baz, el-Baz
(*second reference*); *but* Moammar Gadhafi,
Gadhafi.

  For other names, the article is usually uppercase:
Bordj El Kiffan (city in Algeria)

-elect, president-elect George W. Bush

    —*but* prime minister-designate Jean Chrétien

election day

Elections Canada

Elizabeth Fry Society

Elliot Lake, Ont. (*one t*)

ellipsis, ellipses

E

Elysée Palace
email, electronic mail
embargo, embargoes
embarrass, embarrassment
embassy, Canadian Embassy, Ukrainian Embassy,
     the embassy
embryo, embryos
emcee — *Use* MC
emeritus
     —Jean Duval, professor emeritus of history
emigrant, emigrate, emigration
Emmy, Emmys (TV awards)
emphysema
empire
     —British Commonwealth and Empire, the
     Empire
     —Holy Roman Empire
Empire State Building
employment insurance (*no caps*), EI (*second reference*)
enamour, enamoured (of)
EnCana Corp. (formerly Alberta Energy Co. and
     PanCanadian Energy; TSX:ECA)
encyclopedia
     —*but* Encyclopaedia Britannica
endeavour
Energy Board, National (NEB, *but avoid*)
Engel, Marian (writer, 1933-1985)
England—Do not abbreviate and do not use as
     synonym for Britain.
English Canada, English-Canadian
enormity (wickedness), enormousness (size)
Enquirer, Cincinnati (newspaper)
enquiry — *Use* inquiry
enrol (*not* enroll), enrolled, enrolment
en route (*always two words*)
ensign, the Red Ensign

ensign (rank, *no abbvn.*)
ensure (make sure of)
entomological, entomologist, entomology
entrepreneur, entrepreneurial
Environmental Protection Agency (EPA, *but avoid*)
Epcor Power Limited Partnership (Epcor Power LP
     OK in first reference)
epigram (witty saying), epitaph (inscription on a
     tomb), epithet (descriptive word or phrase)
EpiPen (trademark for epinephrine injector)
equator
ER (emergency room; *OK in second reference*)
Erasmus, Georges
Erickson, Arthur (architect)
Ericsson, Leif (Viking, about 970-1020)
erratum, errata
Eskasoni (Cape Breton First Nations band)
esker (post-glacial gravel)
Eskimo, Eskimos, *but use* Inuk, Inuit
ESL (English as a second language; *explain*)
Esquimalt, B.C.
esthete, esthetic
Eternal City
ethnic-Albanian (*adj.*)
eucharist (holy communion)
euro(s) (EU currency), eight euros, 8.1 euros, 26
     euros
Eurodollar (*no hyphen*)
European Court of Justice
European Parliament (legislative body of EU)
European Union (EU)
euthanasia (*preferred to* mercy killing)
even-steven
everyday (*adj., one word*)
exaggerate, exaggeration
exhilarate

exhort
existence (*not* -ance)
existentialism
exonerate
exorbitant (*not* exhorbitant)
expedite, expediter (*not* -or)
expel, expelled
Expo 67, Expo 86 (*no apostrophe*)
extemporaneous (*not* -eraneous)
extra-bill (*v.*), extra-billing (*n.*)
extracurricular
extraterritorial (*no hyphen*)
extravagant (*not* -ent)
ExxonMobil Corp.
eye, eyeball, eyebrow, eyeful, eyeing, eyelash,
    eyelid, eyesight, eyesore, eyewitness (*no
    hyphens*)
e-zine (Internet magazine)

Facebook
face off (*v.*), faceoff (*n.*)
faculty, faculty of law
FA Cup (Football Association Cup)
    —the Cup competition
Fahd Ibn Abdul Aziz (Saudi Arabia)
    —King Fahd *acceptable in first reference*
Fahrenheit, —20 F (dash, space before F, no period)
Fairmont Hotels & Resorts
fall (season)
fallacious, fallacy
fallible, fallibility
Fallopian tube
fall out (*v.*), fallout (*n.*)
FAQ(s) (frequently asked question(s))
Far East
farmers market *(no apostrophe)*
farm worker(s)
Far North
Farquharson, Charlie (character created by Don
    Harron)
fascism (philosophical attitude)
Fascist (party, member or government)
fascist trends
Father — *Use* Rev. as title for Catholic priest
Father's Day (third Sunday in June)
Fathers of Confederation
faux pas
favour, favourite, favourable
fax (*n.* and *v.*)
faze (disconcert), phase (stage)
federal
    —federal election
    —federal government
Federal Bureau of Investigation (FBI)
Federal Communications Commission (FCC, *but*

F

avoid)
Federal Court
Federal Energy Administration (FEA, *but avoid*)
Federation of Canadian Municipalities (*no abbvn.*)
feedback (*n., no hyphen*)
feisty
fellow, fellowship
    —Nieman Fellowship
ferris wheel (*lowercase*)
fervour
fetal alcohol syndrome
Fête nationale (Quebec holiday on June 24, also
    St-Jean-Baptiste Day)
fettuccine
fetus (*not* foetus)
Feux follets, the (*no hyphen* — dance group)
fever, Lassa fever, spring fever
fiancé (man), fiancée (woman)
Fiberglas (trademark for fibreglass or glass fibre)
field, a polo field
    —Soldier Field
field marshal (*no abbvn.*)
fiery, fierier, fieriest
Fife wheat, Red Fife wheat
Fifth Estate, The (TV program)
fighter-bomber
Fig Newton (trademark for cookies)
Filion, Hervé (harness racing)
Filipino (male), Filipina (female), Filipinos
filmgoer, filmmaker
fiord
fire, fire department, firearm, firebrand, firebomb,
    firecracker, firefighter, fireplace
first lady (U.S. president's wife, *but avoid*)
first lieutenant (1st Lt.)
first ministers conference, meeting

First Nation(s)
First World War (*not* World War I)
50 Cent (rapper)
fivepins (bowling)
flack (press agent), flak (anti-aircraft fire)
flag-bearer
Flags—Capitalize the names of flags and ensigns.
   —Fleur-de-lis, Maple Leaf, Red Ensign, Rising
   Sun, Stars and Stripes, Tricolour, Union Jack
flair (talent), flare (flame, widening)
flak (anti-aircraft fire), flack (press agent)
flamboyant (*no* u)
flamingo, flamingos
flammable (*prefer to* inflammable)
flare up (*v.*), flare-up (*n.*)
flatcar
flaunt (show off), flout (mock)
flavour
fleet
   —the U.S. fleet (whole navy)
   —U.S. Pacific Fleet (formation)
   —Fleet Air Arm (Royal Navy)
Fleming, Sir Sandford (1827-1915)
fleur-de-lis (*not* -lys), Fleur-de-lis (flag)
flexibility, flexible
flight lieutenant (Flight Lieut.)
Flight 132 (*capitalize*)
flight sergeant (Flight Sgt.)
floe (floating sheet of ice)
Florida (Fla.)
flotation (*not* float-)
flounder (thrash about), founder (sink)
flout (mock), flaunt (show off)
FLQ (Front de libération du Québec)
flu (*no apostrophe*)
flutist

flyer (*not* flier), fly-fishing, flyleaf, flypast, fly
　　swatter (*two words*), flyweight, flywheel,
　　frequent flyer
Flying Dutchman (sailboat)
flying officer (*no abbvn.*)
FM (frequency modulation)
FN (for Fabrique nationale) rifle
focus, focused, focuses, focusing
folksinger, folksong
followup (*n.* and *adj.*)
Food and Drugs (*not* Drug) Act
foofaraw
foot-and-mouth disease (*not* hoof-)
Football—backup centre, ball carrier, ball club,
　　blitz (*n., v.*), bootleg, end line, end zone,
　　field goal, fourth-and-one (*adj.*), fullback,
　　goal-line, goal-line stand, halfback, halftime,
　　handoff, kick off (*v.*), kickoff (*n., adj.*), left
　　guard, linebacker, lineman, nose tackle, out of
　　bounds (*adv.*), out-of-bounds (*adj.*), pitchout
　　(*n.*), place kick, placekicker, play off (*v.*),
　　playoff (*n., adj.*), quarterback, runback (*n.*),
　　running back, tailback, tight end, touchback,
　　touchdown
forbear (refrain from), forbearance; forebear
　　(ancestor)
force-feeding
Forces, the; Canadian Forces; the Forces (capped for
　　Canadian only)
forego (precede), foregone; forgo (go without),
　　forgone
Foreign Legion
Foreign Office (U.K.)
forerunner
foresaw, foresee, foreseeable, foreseen
foreword (in a book)

forfeit, forfeiture
forgivable (*not* -eable), forgive
forgo (go without), forgone; forego (precede),
    foregone
format
former
    —former King (Canada, U.K.)
    —former king (other nations)
    —former president George Bush
    —former prime minister Brian Mulroney
    —former Speaker John Fraser
    —former senator Robert de Cotret
Formica (trademark for a laminated plastic)
formula, formulas
Formula One (auto racing), F1 (*OK in second
    reference*)
Forrester, Maureen (contralto)
Fort Chipewyan, Alta.
Fort Frances, Ont.
Fort Macleod, Alta.
Fort McMurray, Alta.
Fort Qu'Appelle, Sask.
Fortran (for formula translation)
founder (sink), flounder (thrash about)
Four Seasons Hotels Inc. (TSX:FSH)
Fourth Estate (press)
Fourth of July, July Fourth (U.S. holiday)
foxtrot (*one word*)
FPinfomart
fracas
francization (*not* -isation — *but preferably avoid*)
Franco-Manitoban
Franco-Ontarian
francophone (*lowercase*)
Francophonie, la (French-speaking equivalent of the
    Commonwealth)

F

freebie (free trip or other benefit)

freelance (*n.*, *v.* and *adj.*); freelancer (*n.*)

Freemason (*one word*)

freestyle swimming

french bread, french door, french fries, french-fried
    potatoes

French Canada, French-Canadian
    —French-speaking Canadian

French Revolution

frequency modulation (FM)

fresco, frescoes

Freudian

Friedan, Betty (feminist, 1921-2006)

Frigidaire (trademark for appliances)

Frisbee (trade name)

Frobisher Bay — *Use* Iqaluit, Nunavut

Front, the (off Newfoundland)

Front de libération du Québec (FLQ)

frontman (*one word*)

front-runner

Fry, Hedy (politician)

Fry, Elizabeth Fry Society

Frye, Northrop (scholar, 1912-1991)

FTP (for file transfer protocol)

Fudgsicle (trademark)

Fuehrer, the (leader; used by Adolf Hitler)

fuel, fuelled, fuelling, fuel cell, fuel injection

-ful (*suffix*), boxful, careful, cheerful, cupful(s),
    handful(s), harmful, spoonful(s), thoughtful,
    useful

fulfil (*not* fulfill), fulfilled, fulfilment

full time, a full-time job, working full time

fulsome (pejorative term, meaning excessive)

Fundamentalist Church of Jesus Christ of Latter Day
    Saints (This group, which embraces polygamy,
    should not be referred to as Mormon or Mormon

fundamentalists, which implies a relationship with the Church of Jesus Christ of Latter-day Saints (Mormons).

fundraiser, fundraising, fundraise

fungus, fungi

furor (*not* furore)

fusilier (*no abbvn.*)

—Fusilier Georges Coté

futile, futilely, futility

F-word is used if said that way in a quote.

FX (movie special effects; spell out *in first reference*)

G

Gadhafi, Moammar
gaff (spar; fish-landing stick); gaffe (faux pas)
Gagnon, Christiane (politician)
gaiety
Gallup poll
Game Boy (two words); GameCube (one word)
Gandhi (*not* Ghandi)
Gap (retailer)
garnishee (*v.* — preferable to garnish)
Gastown (in downtown Vancouver)
Gatineau, Que. (formerly Hull)
GATT (General Agreement on Tariffs and Trade)
gaucho, gauchos
gauge
gauntlet (*not* gantlet)
Gaza Strip
gefilte fish
geiger counter
Geiger-Torel, Herman (opera, 1907-1976)
genealogist
general (Gen.)
    —chief of the general staff
    —Gen. Charles de Gaulle
    —Gen. William Worth
General—In compounds, hyphenate general when
    it is the key word: major-general. Otherwise:
    attorney general, auditor general, governor
    general, secretary general.
General Agreement on Tariffs and Trade (GATT)
General Assembly (of UN)
    —*but* general assembly of the United Church
generation X, generation Xers, generation Y
    —*but* gen-Xer, gen-Y girl
genetically modified (GM, *but avoid*)
Geneva Convention (for one); Geneva Conventions
    (all four)

Genghis Khan (c. 1162-1227)

Genie (movie award)

genius, geniuses

gentile

genus, genera

Geographical Terms—Capitalize regions but not mere direction or position. Capitalize Lake, River, Mountain, Strait, County, etc., when preceding or following the specific term; *but* lowercase the common-noun part of names in plural uses: Ottawa and St. Lawrence rivers, lakes Huron and Superior.

geographic information system (*lowercase;* GIS *OK in second reference)*

George Cross (GC), Medal (GM)

Georges Bank (fishing)

George Town (Bahamas, Malaysia, Tasmania —most others are Georgetown, *but* check)

George Weston Ltd. (TSX:WN)

Georgia (Ga.)

germane

German measles

Germany, Germanys

Gerussi, Bruno (actor, 1928-1995)

get together (*v.*), get-together (*n.*)

G-force

Ghanaian

ghetto, ghettos

ghoul, ghoulish

Gielgud, Sir John (actor, 1904-2000)

gigabyte (GB — *sing.* and *pl.* metric symbol)

gigahertz (GHz; *avoid or include explanation*: one billion cycles a second)

gigolo, gigolos

gillnet, gillnetter

girlfriend, boyfriend

Girl Guides of Canada (association)
    —a girl guide, a guide
    —the Girl Guides, the Guides (association)
    —the Girl Guides movement
    —Brownie
    —Spark
    —Pathfinder
GIS (*Use* geographic information system *in first reference*)
Gitxsan-Wet'suwet'en
Giuseppe (Italian for Joseph)
gizmo, gizmos
gladiolus, gladioli
glamour (*but* glamorous, glamorize)
glasnost
GlaxoSmithKline
global positioning system (*lowercase;* GPS *OK in second reference)*
    Globe and Mail, the Globe and Mail
    —in bylines only, *uppercase* the:
    By Greg Keenan
    The Globe and Mail
GNP (gross national product)
goalkeeper, goalmouth, goalpost, goaltender (*one word*), *but* goal-line (hyphen)
gobbledygook
God—Capitalize sacred names and the proper names and nicknames of the devil: God, Allah, Yahweh, the Almighty, the Father, Jesus Christ, the Son, the Lamb of God, the Saviour, our Lord, Holy Spirit, Trinity, the Prophet (Muhammad), Virgin Mary, Archangel Michael, Angel Gabriel, Satan, Lucifer, Old Nick.
Capitalize He, Him, His, Thou, Thee, Thine, You, Your in reference to the Deity. But lowercase

who, whom, whose.

god (idol)

godchild, godfather, godmother

God damn, God damned (*not* goddam) — *Use with discretion.*

godsend

Gods Lake, Man.

Goebbels, Josef (1897-1945)

Goering, Hermann (1893-1946)

gofer

go-go

goitre

Golden Horseshoe (Oshawa to St. Catharines, Ont.)

Golf—birdie (1 under par), bogey (1 over par; bogeys, bogeyed), double bogey, triple-bogey 7, eagle (2 under par), par 4, par-4 hole, three-wood, No. 3 wood, 1 over par for the round, shot a 1-over-par 73, Canadian Open, Canadian Professional Golfers' Association (CPGA), the Canadian Tour, Ladies Professional Golf Association (LPGA), Masters tournament, PGA Tour, Royal Canadian Golf Association (RCGA), Champions Tour (senior PGA tour)

gonif (thief; clever person; prankster)

gonorrhea

goodbye (*no hyphen*)

Good Friday

Good Samaritan

goodwill (*n.* and *adj.*)

Google, Googled, Googling (*uppercase*)

GOP (U.S. Republican party, *but avoid*)

gorilla

Gortex (trademark for fabric)

gospel, the Four Gospels

—the Gospels

—the Gospel of St. Luke
—the gospel truth
—a gospel singer
got (*not* gotten)
Goteborg (*not* Gothenburg)
Goth (Germanic tribe); goth (subculture)
Gothic (architectural style) *but* a gothic novel
GO Transit, GO train (for Government of Ontario)
Gould, Glenn (pianist, 1932-1982)
Gouzenko, Igor (Soviet defector, 1919-1982)
Government—Capitalize national legislative
bodies, including some short forms.
—House of Commons, Commons
—House of Lords, Lords
—House of Representatives, House
—Bundestag, Diet, Knesset
Lowercase provincial legislatures and their
equivalents and county or city councils.
—Manitoba legislature
—Quebec national assembly
—Toronto city council
governor, governor-in-council (cabinet)
—Gov. Julius Mason
—former governor Anne Lewcyk
—Bank of Canada governor David Dodge
Governor General—Capitalize in all references to
the Canadian incumbent; otherwise only as a
title preceding a name.
—Gov. Gen. Michaëlle Jean
—the Governor General (Canada)
—the governor general (others)
—former governor general Ed Schreyer
—governors general (*pl.*)
—Governor General's Awards, Governor
General's Literary Awards (*never* GG or GGs)
—Governor General's Horse Guards,

Governor General's Foot Guards
GPS (global positioning system)
Grade 7 — *Use* numerals; *but* seventh grade
graffito, graffiti
Graham, Katharine (Washington Post, 1917-2001)
Grain—Capitalize variety names generally except
 where usage has established the lowercase.
  —Thatcher, Selkirk, Rescue
  —*but* durum, garnet, Alberta red winter, No.
  1 northern
grain grower
grain handler
Grammy, Grammys (record awards)
Granada (Spanish city), Grenada (island in the
 Caribbean)
Grand Canyon
granddaughter, great-granddaughter
Grande Prairie, Alta.
Grande Prairie Herald-Tribune
grand jury
grandmaster (bridge and chess)
Grand Prix racing
  —Canadian Grand Prix auto race
Grands ballets canadiens, les; les Grands
grassroots (*one word*)
Gray, Herb (chair, International Joint Commission)
Greater Toronto Area (Toronto and surrounding
 urban regions; GTA *but avoid*)
great-grandfather, great-grandmother
Great-West Lifeco Inc. (TSX:GWO)
Green Berets
Greene, Lorne (actor, 1915-1987)
Greene, Graham (novelist, 1904-1991)
Greenly Island
green movement (environmentalists); Green party
green paper (a tentative report of government

proposals)
Greenpeace Foundation
—Greenpeace V (vessel)
Greenwich Village
Greer, Germaine (feminist)
Greetings—Capitalize common specific greetings:
Merry Christmas, Happy New Year, Happy
Birthday; *but* season's greetings.
Grenada (island in the Caribbean), Granada
(Spanish city)
Grenfell, Sir Wilfred (1865-1940)
Gretzky, Wayne
Grey, Earle (arts award)
Grey, Earl (governor general, Grey Cup)
Grey, Deborah (politician)
grey (colour)
Grey Cup (football)
Grey Panthers
grey whale
grippe
grisly (gruesome), grizzly (bear)
Grit (Liberal)
gross domestic product (GDP)
gross national product (GNP)
groundbreaking
groundcrew (aviation — *one word)*
Groundhog Day (Feb. 2)
groundswell (*one word*)
Ground Zero (New York City), ground zero (other
uses)
group captain (Group Capt. Ed Moir)
Group of Seven (artists), G7, G8 (countries)
grown-up (*n.* and *adj.*)
grow-op(s)
GST (*acceptable in first reference* for goods and
services tax)

G

guacamole
Guantanamo Bay
guardsman (*no abbvn.; but* coastguardman)
guerrilla
guide, a girl guide
    —Girl Guides of Canada (association)
    —the Guides
Guinness (stout)
    —Arthur Guinness, Son and Co. (Dublin) Ltd.
    —Guinness World Records
Guinness, Sir Alec (1914-2000)
Guitar Hero (video game)
Gulf of Aqaba
Gulf Stream
gun, Bren gun, Sten gun
gunfight
gung-ho
gunner (*no abbvn.*)
gunnery sergeant (Gunnery Sgt.)
Guns—Rifles, pistols and other small arms are
    usually described in calibre, expressed in
    decimal fractions of an inch or in metric.
    The word calibre is not used with metric
    measurements. Shotguns are measured in
    gauge.
    —M-16 rifle, 75-mm gun, 12-gauge shotgun,
    .410-bore shotgun, .45-calibre automatic, 30-30
    rifle, .22-calibre rifle
gunship
gunwale
Gurkha (*not* Ghurka)
gurney
guttural (*not* -eral)
Gwich'in (aboriginal band)
Gyllenhaal, Jake and Maggie (actors)
gynecologist, gynecology

G

Gypsy, Gypsies (race of nomadic peoples; *prefer*
Roma)
—*but* gypsy moth, gypsy cab
Gzowski, Peter (broadcaster, 1934-2002)

H

H—Four words and their derivatives begin with silent "h" — heir, honest, honour and hour — requiring "an": an honest man. Otherwise: a historic battle, a hotel.

Haagen-Dazs (ice cream)

habeas corpus (writ)

Habsburg (*not* Hapsburg) Empire

Hague, The

Haida (*sing.* and *pl.*)

hail, hailstone, hailstorm

Hailey, Arthur (novelist, 1920-2004)

hair's-breadth

hajj (Muslim pilgrimage)

hakapik (club used in seal hunt)

halal (food allowed under Muslim law)

half-, halfback, half-baked, half-hour, halfpipe (snowboarding), halftime, halftone (engraving), halves (*pl.*), halfway, halfwit, halfwitted

half, one-half
 —half a dozen
 —a half-dozen

half-mast (*not* half-staff)

Halifax Chronicle-Herald

Haligonian (resident of Halifax)

hall, city hall, firehall
 —Massey Hall
 —Roy Thomson Hall
 —Toronto City Hall

Halley's comet

Hall of Fame

Halloween (*no apostrophe*)

Hamburger Helper (trademark for dinner mix)

Hamilton (specify if not Ontario)

Hamilton Tiger-Cats (*but* Ticats)

handcuff (*v.*), handcuffs (*pl. n.*)

H

Handel, George Frideric (composer, 1685-1759)
handful, handfuls
handgun
hand-held (*n.* and *adj.*)
handmade
H&R Block Ltd. (*no periods; no spaces*)
handshake (*no hyphen*)
hangar (aircraft), hanger (clothes, etc.)
hang-up (*n.*)
Hannover, Germany
Hanukkah
Hapsburg — *Use* Habsburg
hara-kiri
harass, harassing, harassment
harbour, Victoria harbour
hard line, hardline policy, hardliner
harebrained
Hare Krishna, Hare Krishnas
HarperCollins Canada Ltd. (publishers)
Harper's Magazine
Harris, Lawren (painter, 1885-1970)
Harris-Decima (polling company)
Harrods (London store)
Harron, Don (actor)
Hart Memorial Trophy, Hart Trophy (hockey)
hat trick
Havel, Vaclav
Hawaii (*no abbvn.*), Hawaiian
HDTV (*OK in first reference* for high-definition
      television)
headdress
Headingley, Man.
headquarters (*usually takes a plural verb*)
Heads—Capitalize principal words in headings of
      tables, lists and other tabular matter.
head start

heads-up
health care (*n.*) health-care (*adj.*)
hearsay
hearse
heat wave (*two words*)
heaven
heavy water
Hec Crighton Trophy
Hegira, the (Muhammad's)
Heimlich manoeuvre
helix, helixes
hell
Hello (*not* Hello!) magazine
Hells Angels (*no apostrophe*), Angels (*second
        reference*)
helter-skelter
hemisphere
        —Western Hemisphere
hemophilia
hemorrhage
Hennessy, Jill (actor)
hepatitis A, B, C
herculean (*lowercase*)
hero, heroes (*pl.*)
heyday (*no hyphen*)
Hezbollah (Party of God)
hiccup, hiccuped
hide-and-seek, hideaway, hideout
hieroglyph, hieroglyphs (*n.*); hieroglyphic (*adj.*),
        hieroglyphics (*n., pl.*)
High Arctic
highbrow (*no hyphen*)
high commissioner, High Commissioner Lauren
        Chow
high definition *(n.)*, high-definition TV *(adj.)* (HD or
        HDTV *acceptable in second reference*)

H

highlight (*no hyphen*)
high mass
highrise
high-tech
highway
>—the highway to Paris
>—Highway 27
>—Trans-Canada Highway

hijab
hijinks
Hill, the (informal for Parliament Hill)
hindrance
Hindu, Hinduism
hip hop *(n.)*, hip-hop music *(adj.)*
hippie, hippies
hippopotamus, hippopotamuses
Hirsch, John (1930-1989)
His—Capitalize His in reference to the Deity,
His (or Her) Majesty, His (or Her) Royal
Highness, His Holiness, His Grace, His
Honour, His Lordship, His Worship. But use
such terms of address only in quotations.
>—His Worship Mayor Phillips
>—and His Worship said ...
>—His Royal Highness, the Prince of Wales

Hispanic
historic (important or outstanding in history)
>—historical (about history)
>—a (*not* an) historical site

Historical Eras—Capitalize historical periods and
events, including widely recognized popular
names: Pliocene Epoch, Stone Age, Iron Age,
Exodus, Ming Dynasty, Dark Ages, Middle
Ages, Hundred Years War, Renaissance,
American Civil War, Prohibition, Great
Depression, Roaring '20s, Dirty '30s, Beer Hall

Putsch, Holocaust, Space Age, Me Decade; *but* ice age (no single period)

—21st century

History Television (Canada), History (U.S.)

hitchhike, hitchhiking (*no hyphen*)

Hitler, Adolf (*not* Adolph) (1889-1945)

HIV (for human immunodeficiency virus)

—HIV-positive

—HIV-AIDS

Ho Chi Minh City (Vietnam), Ho Chi Minh Trail

Hockey—blue-line, face off (*v.*), faceoff (*n., adj.*), goalie, goal-line, goalmouth, goalpost, goals-against average, goaltender, left-wing pass, left-winger, play off (*v.*), playoff (*n., adj.*), power play, power-play goal, red-line, right-winger, short-handed (*adj.*), shut out (*v.*), shutout (*n., adj.*), slapshot

Hockey Canada (governing body of amateur hockey in Canada)

hodgepodge (*no hyphen*)

Hodgkin's disease

Hogtown (nickname for Toronto)

hold up (*v.*), holdup (*n.*)

hole, buttonhole, pigeonhole

Holidays—Capitalize religious holidays and feasts and all special times: Christmas Eve, Easter, Hanukkah, Yom Kippur, Ramadan, New Year's Day, Father's Day.

Hollinger Inc.

Holocaust (murder by Nazis of six million Jews), holocaust (all other meanings)

Holt, Renfrew and Co. Ltd.

—*but* Holt Renfrew (no comma)

Holy Father (the Pope, *but avoid*)

Holy Grail (chalice Christ drank from); grail (any quest)

H

Holy Land

Holy See (Vatican)

Holy Week

home, homebrew, homebuilder, homebuyer, home field (*n.*), home-field (*adj.*), homegrown, homemade, homeowner, home page (*two words*), homesick, hometown, homework

homey (*not* homy)

Hong Kong Special Administrative Region, People's Republic of China (formal name, Hong Kong *OK in all references*)

honky-tonk (*hyphen*)

honour, honourable *but* honorary

hoodie (hooded sweatshirt)

hoof, hoofs

Hook of Holland

hoopla

horseback (*one word*)

Horse Racing—race card, racecourse, racehorse, racetrack, raceway.

hospital, hospital commission
    —Shaughnessy Hospital
    —St. John's General Hospital
    —Hospital for Sick Children
    —Laval hospital commission

hot, hotbox, hotcake, hotdog, hotfoot, hothead, hothouse, hotline (show, *prefer* open-line), Hotmail (trademark, *uppercase*), hotplate, hotrod, hotshot (all one word); *but* hot air, hot-blooded, hot cross bun, hot potato, hot spot, hot water

hotel
    —Royal York Hotel
    —Fairmont Hotel Vancouver
    —a Vancouver hotel

House of Commons (Canadian and British)

—the House, the Commons
—the lower house (Commons)
—House leader Jean Roy (federal)
—the house (provincial)
—house leader Jean Roy (provincial)
hovercraft
—SRN-6 hovercraft
—British Hovercraft Corp.
HPV (human papillomavirus; *OK in first reference but include full term elsewhere*)
HSBC Bank Canada
HTML (Hypertext Markup Language)
hubbub
Hudson Bay
Hudson's Bay Co., the Bay (store), HBC (corporate entity)
Hudson's Hope, B.C.
Hu Jintao, Hu *(second reference)*
hullabaloo
human papillomavirus (HPV *OK in first reference but use full term elsewhere*)
Human Resources and Social Development Canada
humdinger
humdrum *(no hyphen)*
humongous
humour *but* humorous, humorist
Humvee (military vehicle), Hummer (civilian version)
Huntington's disease
hurricane Hazel
Hush Puppies (trademark for casual shoes)
Hussein, Saddam (1937-2006), Saddam *(second reference)*
Hutterites
hydroelectric *(no hyphen)*
Hydro-Québec *(hyphen)*

H

hyperlink
hypocrisy, hypocrite
hypothesis, hypotheses
hysterectomy
Hyundai Auto Canada Inc.
    —Hyundai Corp. (parent company)

Iacocca, Lee
I-beam
ice age (no single period)
icebreaker (*no hyphen*)
ice cream, ice-cream bar
icewine (*one word*)
ICU (*OK for* intensive care unit *in second reference*)
ID (identification, *no periods)*
Idaho (*no abbvn.*)
idiosyncrasy
i.e. (*prefer* that is)
IED (use improvised explosive device *in first reference*)
IGM Financial Inc. (TSX:IGM)
      —Investors Group Inc.
      —Mackenzie Financial Corp.
Ignatieff, Michael
Ikea (*not* IKEA)
Iles-de-la-Madeleine
ill, ill feeling, ill will; *but* ill-fated, ill-mannered, ill-starred
Illecillewaet, B.C.
Illinois (Ill.)
illusion (false impression), allusion (indirect reference)
imam, Imam Aly Hindy
Imax (big-screen movies)
imitator (*not* -er)
immanent (pervading, inherent), imminent (impending)
Immigration and Refugee Board
immovable (*not* -eable)
imperial, imperial measure
Imperial Oil Ltd. (TSX:IMO)
impetus, impetuses
implement (*n*. and *v*.), implementation

impostor (*not* -er)

impresario (*not* -ss-)

impressionism (school of art), impressionistic style

improvised explosive device (IED *OK in second reference*)

in, inbound, indoor, in-depth, infighting, in-group, in-house, in-law; break-in, cave-in, stand-in, walk-in, write-in

inaccessible (*not* -able)

inadmissible (*not* -able)

inadvertent (*not* -ant)

inauguration day *(lowercase)*

inbox (mail)

income tax
> —income tax deduction

incompatibility, incompatible

Incorporated—*Use* Inc. in business names.

incorruptible (*not* -able)

Independence Day (U.S.)

independent, Independent (MP), Ind *(abbvn., no period)*

in depth, in-depth *(adj.)*

index, indexes
> —Dow Jones industrial average
> —S&P/TSX composite index

Indiana (Ind.)

indict, indictable

indigenous

indispensable (*not* -ible)

Industrial Revolution

Indy-car race

infallible

infantry, 4th Infantry Battalion

infinitesimal

inflammable — *Use* flammable

inflammation, inflammatory

In Flanders Fields (First World War poem by John

McCrae)
information highway (*lowercase*)
Informetrica
infrared
ING Canada Inc. (TSX:IIC)
ingenious (clever), ingenuous (frank, innocent)
inherent
in-line skating
innocuous
innovate, innovation, innovator
Innu (Aboriginal Peoples in Labrador)
innuendo, innuendoes
inoculate, inoculation
inquire, inquiry, inquiries
  —Cincinnati Enquirer
  —Philadelphia Inquirer
Inquisition, Spanish
inscribe (*not* enscribe), inscription
insignia (*sing.* and *pl.*)
insistence (*not* -ance), insistent (*not* -ant)
inspector, Insp. John Smith
install, installation
instalment
instant message, messaging (IM, *but avoid*)
instil, instilled
institute
  —Women's Institute
insure (cover loss)
intefadeh (Palestinian uprising)
intelligence quotient (IQ)
Interac (banking)
Inter-American Development Bank (IDB, *but avoid*)
Inter American Press Association (IAPA, *but avoid*)
intercollegiate (*no hyphen*)
intercontinental (*no hyphen*)
Intercounty Baseball League

interdependence (*no hyphen*)
interfere, interference
interferon (*lowercase*)
Interior, the (B.C.)
interleague (baseball)
intern (hospital)
International Bank for Reconstruction and
    Development (World Bank)
International Civil Aviation Organization (ICAO)
International Court of Justice (*no abbvn.*)
international date line
International Development Association (IDA, *but*
    avoid)
International Grains Arrangement (*no abbvn.*)
International Joint Commission (IJC, *but avoid*)
International Labour Organization (ILO)
International Monetary Fund (IMF)
International Space Station (ISS, *but avoid*)
International Telecommunications Satellite
    Consortium (Intelsat *OK in first reference*)
International Wheat Agreement, the agreement
Internet—Capitalize specific proper names.
    —Internet
    —World Wide Web, *but* the web
    —Adobe Acrobat, JavaScript
    Lowercase descriptive or generic terms.
    —electronic mail, email
    —blog, chat room, cyberspace, domain name,
    home page, hyperlink, instant messaging,
    shareware
    —web, web browser, webcam, webcast,
    web-enabled, webmaster, web page, web
    server, website
    Use all caps for well-known acronyms and
    abbreviations.
    —CD-ROM, FTP, HTML, HTTP (but

I

lowercase in web addresses), PDF, RAM, URL
If providing an Internet address, follow upper
and lowercase of actual address. Include
www if appropriate: www.thecanadianpress.
com.
If a company uses a variation of its Internet
address as its corporate name, capitalize the
first word: Amazon.com.
interpreter (*not* -or)
interracial (*no hyphen*)
intervene, intervener (*not* -or)
Intracoastal Waterway (*not* Inter-)
intranet (*lowercase*)
Inuit Tapiriit Kanatami (Inuit organization, means
Inuit are united in Canada)
Inuk (*sing. n.* and *adj.*), Inuit (*pl. n.* and *adj.*)
Inukshuk (stone figure)
Inuktitut (language)
inundate, inundation
Inuvialuit (western Arctic aboriginals)
Inuvik, N.W.T.
Iowa (*no abbvn.*)
IPO (initial public offering; *OK in first reference* in
business copy)
iPod (Capitalize lowercase names at the beginning
of a sentence: IPod.)
Ipsco Inc. (TSX:IPS)
Ipsos-Reid (polling company)
Iqaluit, Nunavut
IRA (Irish Republican Army)
iridescent
Irish Republican Army (IRA)
Iron Curtain (outmoded term)
ironic, ironically (*use advisedly*; it does not mean
coincidentally)
irrelevant

irreparable
irresistible (*not* -able)
irreverent (*not* -ant)
island
 —Vancouver Island
 —the Island (informal for Vancouver Island and P.E.I.)
Ismailia (*not* Ismailiya)
Ispat Sidbec Inc. (former Quebec steel company; now Mittal Canada Inc.)
IT (for information technology; *spell out*)
Itar-Tass news agency
it's (it is, it has; similar to he's, she's)
 —its (possessive; similar to his, hers)
iTunes
IUD (acceptable on first reference for intra-uterine device)
Ivy League

jackhammer

jack pine

Jackson's Point, Ont.

Jacuzzi (trademark for whirlpool tub)

Jaffer, Rahim (politician)

jail (facility, usually provincial, where people are
held temporarily or serve sentences of two
years less a day)
   —county jail, jailbird, jailbreak
   —Don Jail (capped when part of formal
   name)

jalabiya (robe-type garment worn in Africa and the
Middle East)

Javex (trademark for bleach)

Jaws of Life (trademark for extraction equipment)

Jaycees International, the Jaycees

Jean, Michaelle

Jean Coutu Group (TSX:PJC.A)

jeep (for the military vehicle), Jeep (for the
trademark sport utility vehicle)

Jeff Russel Trophy (football)

Jehovah

Jehovah's Witnesses
   —a Jehovah's Witness, a Witness

Jell-O (trademark for gelatin dessert)

jerry-built

Jet Ski (trademark for personal watercraft)

JetStar

Jew (for man and woman, *not* Jewess)
   —Reform Jew
   —Orthodox Jew

jeweller, jewelry

Jiang Zemin, Jiang (*second reference*)

Jidda, Saudi Arabia

jihad (Arab noun for struggle to do good; often
used to mean holy war)

J

jodhpurs
john (lavatory; prostitute's customer)
Johns Hopkins Hospital, University
Joint Task Force 2 (Canadian Forces
    counter-terrorism response unit)
joual (Quebec dialect)
Journal de Montréal, Le (newspaper)
Journal de Québec, Le (newspaper)
JTI-Macdonald Corp. (formerly RJR-Macdonald
    Inc.)
Juan Carlos de Borbon
    —Juan Carlos I (king of Spain)
jubilee, Golden Jubilee
judge, Judge Kevin Ward
judgment (*not* judgement)
Juilliard School of Music
jumbo jet (wide-bodied jet plane, including the
    Boeing 747, Lockheed, L-1011, DC-10 and
    Airbus)
junior
    —John Jones Jr. (*no comma*)
Juno Awards, Junos
jury, grand jury
justice (usually reserved for appeal court judges;
    otherwise, use judge)
    —Chief Justice Albert Weisman, Justice Jean
    Dupont, Justice Sadie Kells (*not* Madam
    Justice)
    —Smith or the judge or justice in second
    reference
justice of the peace
    —justice of the peace Jean Isaac

K

Kabul, Afghanistan
Kaczynski, Theodore (unabomber)
kaffeeklatsch
Kahnawake (Que.)
kaiser (roll)
kaiser, Kaiser Wilhelm
kalamata olives
kamikaze
Kampuchea (now Cambodia)
Kandahar, Afghanistan
Kanesatake (Que.)
Kaposi's sarcoma (AIDS-related cancer)
Karadzic, Radovan
karaoke
karat (gold), carat (gems)
   —14-karat gold *(hyphen)*
Karsh, Yousuf (photographer, 1908-2002)
Kathmandu
Kazaa
Kazakhstan
Kejimkujik National Park, N.S.
Kenora Miner and News
Kentucky (Ky.)
kerfuffle
ketchup
Kettle and Stony Point First Nation (Ontario)
keynote (*no hyphen*)
Keystone Kops
KGB (acceptable in all references for the Russian
     words meaning Committee of State Security;
     but include a descriptive phrase such as
     former Soviet secret police)
Khachaturian, Aram (composer, 1903-1978)
khaki
Khan, Genghis (c. 1162-1227)
Khmer Rouge

K

Khomeini, Ayatollah Ruhollah (1902-1989)
Khrushchev, Nikita (1894-1971)
kibbutz (communal farm), kibbutzim (*pl.*),
    kibbutznik (resident)
kibitz, kibitzer
kick back (*v.*), kickback (*n.*), kick off (*v.*), kickoff (*n.*)
kidnap, kidnapped, kidnapper
Kiev — *Use* Kyiv
kilo (*avoid* as an abbreviation for kilogram or
    kilometre)
kilobyte (KB — *sing.* and *pl.* metric symbol)
kilometre (km — *sing.* and *pl.* metric symbol, *no
    period*)
    —km/h
kilowatt hour (kWh — *sing.* and *pl.* metric symbol,
    no period)
Kimberley, B.C.
Kimberly-Clark
kimchee (Korean dish)
kimono, kimonos
kindergarten
King (of the U.K. and Canada), king (other nations)
King, William Lyon Mackenzie (1874-1950)
    —usually just Mackenzie King; King *on second
    reference*
Kingston Whig-Standard
Kinsmen Clubs
Kish, Nehemiah (ballet)
Kiss (*not* KISS) rock group
Kitchener-Waterloo Record — *Use* Waterloo Region
    Record
kitsch
Kitty Litter (trademark for cat litter)
Kiwanis International
Kleenex (trademark for paper tissue)
klieg lights (limelight)

Klondike
Kluane National Park
klutz (a bungler)
km/h (kilometres per hour)
Kmart stores (*not* K-Mart)
Knesset (Israeli parliament)
knick-knack (*hyphen*)
knight
 —Knights of Columbus
 —Knights of Pythias
know-how (*hyphen*)
knowledgeable
knuckleball
Kool-Aid
Kootenai River (U.S.)
Kootenay East, West (B.C. regions)
Kootenay River (B.C.)
Koran — *Use* Qur'an
k-os (hip-hop artist)
Kostunica, Vojislav (Yugoslav politician)
Kosygin, Alexei (1904-1980)
Kouchibouguac National Park, N.B.
kowtow
KPMG LLP (Canadian arm of KPMG International)
Krakow, Poland
Krazy Glue (trademark for instant glue)
krebiozen (cancer drug)
Kreviazuk, Chantal (singer)
Krieghoff, Cornelius (1815-1872)
krona, kronor (Swedish currency)
krona, kronur (Icelandic currency)
krone, kroner (Danish and Norwegian currency)
Kuerti, Anton (pianist)
Ku Klux Klan
kung fu
Kurelek, William (painter, 1927-1977)

K

Kuujjuaq, Que.
Kwanlin Dun First Nation (Yukon)
Kyiv (*not* Kiev)
Kyoto Protocol (*but* Kyoto agreement, accord)
Kyrgyzstan (formerly Kirghizia), Kyrgyz (*n., adj.*)

L.A. (*OK in second reference* for Los Angeles; *use periods*)

La, Le—When lowercase in names, capitalize only at the start of the sentence. Prefer "the" before French names of associations and groups; capitalize "le" or "la" when it is the first word of the title of a book, song, play and the like.

Labatt (part of Belgium-based Interbrew)
> —Labatt Brewing Co.
> —Labatt (*not* Labatt's) announced
> —Labatt's beer

label, labelled

labour *but* laborious

Labour Day (*not* Labor Day)

Labour sympathizer (party)
> —Labour party

labour sympathizer (union)

Labradorian (resident of Labrador)

Labrador Party

Labrador retriever

Lac de Gras, N.W.T.

lacklustre

Lac La Biche, Alta.

Ladies' Home Journal

Lady Byng Trophy (hockey)

Lake—Capitalize as part of a proper name: Eels Lake, Lake Huron. Lowercase in plural use: lakes Erie and Ontario, Eels and Duck lakes.

Lake of the Woods, Ont.

Lake Shore Boulevard (Toronto)

lama (monk), llama (animal)

LaMarsh, Judy (1924-1980)

lambaste, lambaster, lambasting

Lamborghini

landau (horse-drawn carriage)

landline (*one word*)

L

landmine (*one word*)
Land Rover (trademark)
lang, k.d.
L'Annonciation, Que.
laptop (computer)
largemouth (bass)
largesse
larva, larvae
laryngitis
larynx, larynxes
lasagna
laser (for light amplification by stimulated emission
of radiation)
Lassa fever
lasso, lassos
L'Assomption, Que.
Last Spike (driven into railway at Craigellachie,
B.C., on Nov. 7, 1885)
Last Supper
Latin America (*no hyphen*)
laudable
Laumann, Silken (rower)
Laurence, Margaret (author, 1926-1987)
Laurier, Sir Wilfrid (1841-1919)
—Wilfrid Laurier University
Lavigne, Avril (musician)
law
—Law of the Sea conference
lawsuit
Lay—This is an action word; it takes a direct object:
The gunman lays the rifle down, is laying it
down, laid it down, has laid it down, had laid
it down, will lay it down.
lay off (*v.*), layoff (*n.*)
lead (*v.*), led, leading
Leader—Capitalize as a semi-official title when

used with the name of a political party and directly preceding a name.

—NDP Leader Jack Layton

—*but* party leader Jack Layton

—deputy leader Jean Roy

—former Tory leader Joe Clark

—House leader Tony Valeri (federal)

—house leader Claude Littlefeathers (provincial)

—Japanese leader Junichiro Koizumi

leading seaman (*no abbvn.*)

league

—League of Nations

—National Hockey League (NHL)

—American League (baseball)

—Catholic Women's League

leap, leapfrog (*n.* and *v. — no hyphen*), leap year

Learjet (trademark)

LeBreton, Marjory (senator)

le Carré, John (author)

Led Zeppelin

leery (*not* leary)

leeway

left, left field, left-fielder, left wing, left-winger, left-field wall, left-handed pitcher, left-wing politician (*adj., hyphen*)

Left Bank (Paris)

left-handed, left-hander *(hyphens)*

legation, Canadian Legation, the legation

Léger, Paul-émile (1904-1991, former Roman Catholic cardinal

legion

—Foreign Legion

—Royal Canadian Legion, the legion

legionnaire

legionnaires' disease

L

Legislature—Capitalize national legislatures; lowercase others.

—Parliament, House of Commons, Commons, House *but* lower house; Senate *but* upper house; Congress, House of Representatives, House; Chamber of Deputies, Chamber; Knesset, Bundestag, French National Assembly.

—Quebec national assembly, Manitoba legislature, Newfoundland and Labrador house of assembly; legislature, house.

legislature member, member of the legislature

leitmotif

le May Doan, Catriona (speed skater)

lemon grass

lend, lent (*v.*), loan (*n.*)

lenience

Leningrad — *Use* St. Petersburg

Lent (season)

Leonardo da Vinci (1452-1519), Leonardo (*not* da Vinci) *on second reference*

Leopard 1 (tank)

Lepreau, Point

leukemia

Lévesque, René (1922-1987)

Levi's (trademark for a brand of jeans)

Lewiston Maineiacs (hockey team)

Lhasa, Tibet

liaison

libel, libelled, libellous

liberal (philosophical attitude)

—a liberal education

Liberal (party or member)

—the Liberal party

—Liberal Party of Canada (formal name)

liberty, liberty boat, *but* Liberty ship

—Statue of Liberty

—the Liberty Bell

library, Toronto Public Library, National Library
(capitalize official names)

Libya, Libyan

licence (*n.*), license (*v.*)

licensed, licensee, licensing

Lie—This verb, meaning to recline or be situated,
does not take a direct object: Trudeau lies in
state, is lying in state, lay in state, has lain in
state, had lain in state, will lie in state.

lie (*n.*), lie-detector

Liechtenstein

lieutenant (Lt.)

lieutenant-colonel (Lt.-Col. John Smith)

—lieutenant-colonels

lieutenant-commander (Lt.-Cmdr. Stan Lyubic)

lieutenant-general (Lt.-Gen. Lee Ward)

—lieutenant-generals

lieutenant-governor, lieutenant-governors

—Lt.-Gov. Carole Pelletier

—the lieutenant-governor said ...

life (*prefix*), lifebelt, lifeboat, lifebuoy, life cycle,
lifeguard, life-jacket, lifeless, lifelike, lifeline,
lifelong, life-preserver, life-raft, life-size,
lifespan, lifestyle, life-support, lifetime

Life Saver (trademark for a brand of candy)

life-work

lightface (type)

light heavyweight

lighthouse, lightkeeper

light-year

likable (*not* -eable)

lime, lime-kiln (*hyphen*), limelight (*no hyphen*)

Limey (slang for British, considered offensive,
avoid)

L

Limited—Use Ltd. and ltée (*lowercase, no period*) in business names.

Limited Partnership—LP (*no periods*) *OK in first reference* for business names: Fort Chicago Energy Partners LP.

linage (advertising), lineage (ancestry)

linchpin (*not* lynchpin)

Lincoln Center

line, line 2

lineage (ancestry), linage (number of lines)

lineman (football player), linesman (hockey official)

line up (*v.*), lineup (*n.*)

Lions, Gulf of

Lions Gate Bridge

Lion's Head, Ont.

liquefied natural gas (LNG)

liquefy, liquefier, liquefaction

liqueur

lira, lire (*pl.*)

Listeria (genus), listeriosis (infection)

Listuguj (Mi'kmaq band)

Liszt, Franz (1811-1886)

litre (l — *sing.* and *pl.* metric symbol, *no period*)

Little League Baseball World Series

livable (*not* -eable)

living room

LLD (doctor of laws, *but avoid*)

Lloyd's (insurance market, shipping information)
    —Lloyds Bank (no apostrophe)

Lloyd Webber, Andrew (composer)

loan (*n.*), lend, lent (*v.*)

loan shark (*n. only — two words*)

loath (unwilling), loathe (despise)

Loblaw Cos. Ltd. (TSX:L)
    —Loblaw (corporate reference)
    —Loblaws store, Loblaws (retail outlets)

Local 14 (union)

Locations, Places, Sites—Capitalize the names of
important buildings, residences, historical
and battle sites, universities and colleges,
hospitals and hotels. Capitalize Union Station,
Grand Central Station as important buildings
but not when known by name of railway or
town: the Via Rail station, Leaside station.
Capitalize the names of parks, gardens,
playing fields and arenas. Lowercase post
offices and courthouses.

locker-room

lock out (*v.*), lockout (*n.*)

lock up (*v.*), lockup (*n.*)

lodge, Orange Lodge
—the lodge meeting

log in *(v.)*, login (*n.* and *adj.*)

London Free Press

long (*suffix*), daylong, yearlong *but* hour-long,
month-long, week-long

long distance, a long-distance phone call

long house

Long Island Rail Road

long johns

longliner (fishing vessel)

long-range, a long-range forecast

long-standing, a long-standing rule

long-term (*adj.*)

longtime (*no hyphen*, compound modifier)

Longueuil, Que.

loonie (dollar coin), loony (insane), Looney Tunes
(cartoons)

loophole (*no hyphen*)

looseleaf (*no hyphen*)

loran (for long-range air navigation system)

Lords, the (institution), lords (members), Lord's

(cricket ground)
Lord's Prayer, the
L'Orignal, Ont.
Losier-Cool, Rose-Marie (senator)
Loto-Québec (*hyphen*)
Lotto 6-49
Louisbourg, N.S.
　　　—Fortress of Louisbourg
Louisiana (La.)
Lou Marsh Trophy
lovable (*not* -eable)
lowbrow (*no hyphen*)
Lower Canada (name for southern portion of
　　　Quebec from 1791 to 1840)
lowercase (*n., v.*)
lower house
Lower Mainland (B.C.)
Lower Manhattan (New York City)
Lower Town (Quebec or Ottawa)
LSD (acceptable in all references for lysergic acid
　　　diethylamide)
Luftwaffe
lunch box, lunch bucket
Lunenburg, N.S.
Lutz (figure-skating jump)
Luxembourg
luxury, luxurious
Lycra (trademark for spandex fibre)
Lyme disease

M

MA (master of arts)
    —a master's degree
Macau
MacDonald, J.E.H. (painter, 1873-1932)
Macdonald, Man.
MacDonald, Flora
Macdonald, Sir John A. (1815-1891)
Macdonald, Angus L. (Nova Scotia politician,
    1890-1954; Halifax bridge)
MacDonald, Ann-Marie (writer)
Macdonald-Cartier Freeway, Highway 401
Macdonald College
Mace (trademark for a paralysing spray)
mace (staff of office; club), mace-bearer
MacEachen, Allan (politician)
MacGregor, Man.
Mach (speed, after physicist Ernest Mach)
machiavellian
machine-gun
    —submachine-gun
Macintosh (computer)
    —*but* McIntosh (apple)
MacIsaac, Ashley
MacKay, Peter (politician)
MacKenzie, Lewis
Mackenzie, William Lyon (patriot, 1795-1861;
    grandfather of William Lyon Mackenzie King)
Mackenzie, Alexander (1822-1892)
Mackenzie Highway, River, Valley
mackinaw (cloth, heavy coat)
mackintosh (coat)
Mack Truck (trademark)
MacLean, Ron (sportscaster)
Maclean's magazine
MacLennan, Hugh (author, 1907-1990)
MacMillan, Sir Ernest (1893-1973)

M

Macmillan Canada (former publisher)

MacNeil, Rita (singer)

Macphail, Agnes (Canada's first woman MP, 1890-1954)

Macpherson, Kay (feminist, 1913-1999)

madam (polite form of address; brothel-keeper)

madame (French title of respect)
—Madame Robert Duval (*no abbvn.*)

mad cow disease (*OK in first reference* for BSE)

mademoiselle (*no abbvn.*)

Madonna (performer), the Madonna (mother of Jesus)

Madras, India (now Chennai)

maelstrom

Mafia; Mafioso, Mafiosi (member, *sing.* and *pl.*)

Magazine—Capitalize when part of the actual title.
—New York Times Magazine
—Maclean's magazine
—Time magazine

Magdalen Islands - *Use* Iles-de-la-Madeleine

Magna Carta (*not* Charta)

Magna International Inc. (TSX:MG.A)

Magnum (trademark for a cartridge), a .357-calibre Magnum revolver, a Colt Python .357

mail-order catalogue (*hyphen*)

Maine (*no abbvn.*)

mainframe

major (Maj. Alice Lajoie)

major-general (Maj.-Gen. Kevin Ward), major-generals

make up (*v.*), makeup (*n.*), makeover (*n.*)

malemute (dog)

Mallorca

Mamma Mia (musical, *not* Mamma Mia!)

mammogram, mammography (breast X-ray)

mandarin (civil servant); Mandarin (Chinese

dialect)
manhattan (cocktail)
manhunt
Manila, Philippines
manila paper
Manitoba (Man.)
Manitoba Telecom Services Inc. (TSX:MBT)
manoeuvre
Man of the Year
man-of-war (warship)
    —Man o' War (racehorse)
mantel (fireplace)
mantle (cloak)
Manulife Financial Corp. (TSX:MFC)
Mao Zedong, Mao (*second reference*)
    —Maoism
maple leaf, leaves
    —Maple Leaf (flag, emblem)
    —Toronto Maple Leafs
Maple Leaf Foods Inc. (TSX:MFI)
Maple Leaf Gardens
March (*no abbvn.*)
march past (*n.* and *v.*)
Mardi Gras
marijuana
marine, marine corps
    —U.S. Marine Corps
    —Royal Marines
    —a marine, the marines, marine offensive, etc.
maritime
    —Maritime provinces, the Maritimes
    —New Brunswick, Nova Scotia, P.E.I.
    —The Atlantic provinces comprise the
    Maritimes and Newfoundland and Labrador.
Maritime Employers Association (MEA, *but avoid*)
Mark, Inky (politician)

M

marketplace
Mark III, Mark 46 (follow maker's style)
Marks & Spencer
Marleau, Diane (politician)
marquess *but* Marquis of Queensberry rules
Marquis wheat
Marrakech (*not* Marrakesh)
Marseille
marshal (*n.* and *v.*), marshalled, fire marshal, parade
    marshal
Marshall Plan
martini
Martyrs' Shrine (at Midland, Ont.)
marvellous
Marxism, Marxist
Maryland (Md.)
Mase (rap singer)
MASH
Mason (member of Masonic order)
mason (person who builds with stone)
Masonite (a trademark for a brand of hardboard)
Mason jar
mass, low mass, high mass, requiem mass
Massachusetts (Mass.)
massasauga (rattlesnake)
mastectomy
MasterCard
master corporal (Master Cpl. Pierre Charest)
masterful (domineering), masterly (skilful)
master of arts (MA), a master's degree
master of ceremonies (MC)
Masters, the (golf tournament)
master seaman (*no abbvn.*)
master sergeant (Master Sgt.)
master warrant officer (*no abbvn.*)
matchup (*n.*), match up (*v.*)

M

matrix, matrixes
matzo, matzos
maximum, maximums
mayday (distress signal)
mayonnaise
mayor, Mayor Grace McDonald
> —the mayor of Ottawa
> —former mayor Ken Elman
> —acting mayor Ken Elman
> —the acting mayor
> —mayor-elect Ken Elman
> —Deputy Mayor Patrick Keenan (formal title)

mayoralty (*n.*), mayoral (*adj.*)
mazel tov (good luck)
MC (master of ceremonies), MCs, MCing, MCed,
> *but use only* when meaning is clear from
> context

McCarthy, Joseph (U.S. senator, 1945-1957)
McCarthy Tétrault (legal firm)
McClelland & Stewart Ltd. (publisher)
McClung, Nellie (feminist, 1873-1951)
McCrae, John (1872-1918, poet who wrote *In
> Flanders Fields*)
McDonald's Restaurants of Canada Ltd.
> —McDonald's
McDonnell Douglas Canada Ltd.
McDonough, Alexa (politician)
McEntire, Reba (singer)
McGraw-Hill Ryerson Ltd. (publisher)
McIntosh apple
> —*but* Macintosh (computer)
McLachlan, Sarah (singer)
McLachlin, Beverley (Supreme Court chief justice)
McLaren, Norman (filmmaker, 1914-1987)
McLauchlan, Murray (folksinger)
McLaughlin, Audrey (former NDP leader)

M

McLuhan, Marshall (1911-1980)

M'Clure Strait (in Arctic); named after explorer Sir
Robert M'Clure (1807-73)

McPherson, Aimee Semple (evangelist, 1890-1944)

MDS Inc. (TSX:MDS)

meagre (*not* -ger)

Meals on Wheels

meat packer (*two words*) *but* meat-packing

Mecca (place)
—*but* a music mecca

medal, medallist

Medals—Capitalize specific names.
—Medal of Bravery
—the Military Medal
—a military medal

medevac

Medicaid (U.S. program of health care for poor)

medicare (government medical insurance plan in
general), Medicare (U.S. health program)

medieval

Mediterranean

medium, media (*pl.* — except mediums in
spiritualism)

Meech Lake accord

meerschaum (pipe)

megapixel (*avoid* MP)

Mehta, Deepa (filmmaker)

member
—member of Parliament (MP, MPs)
—member of the Order of the British Empire
(MBE)
—member of provincial parliament
(MPP — Ontario only, *but avoid*)
—member of house of assembly
(MHA — N.L. only, *but avoid*)
—member of legislative assembly

M

(MLA, *but avoid*)
—member of national assembly
(MNA — Quebec only, *but avoid*)
memento, mementoes
memo, memos
memoir (*not* memoire)
—*but* aide-mémoire
memorandum, memorandums
Mendelssohn, Felix (composer, 1809-1847)
meningitis, meningococcal disease
Mennonite
menswear, womenswear
mentally retarded — *Avoid* as sometimes
   considered offensive. *Use* mentally
   handicapped.
Mentv (specialty channel)
Mercator projection
Mercedes-Benz
merchant marine
Messiah, a messiah
Messrs. — *Use* Messieurs (before names)
meter (gauge)
methadone
Métis (mixed Indian and European ancestry)
metre (m — *sing.* and *pl.* metric symbol, *no period*);
   but diameter
metrication (*not* metrification)
Metro Inc. (TSX:MRU.A)
Mexico City
MHA (N.L. only — member of house of assembly,
   but avoid)
Michigan (Mich.)
mickey (half-sized bottle of liquor)
Micmac — *Use* Mi'kmaq
micro (*prefix*), microbrewery, microsurgery,
   microwave, micro-organism

M

microphone, mike
microwaveable
midday
Middle (*not* Near) East
Middle Ages
Middle West, Midwest (U.S.)
Mideast
midshipman (*no abbvn.*)
midsummer (*no hyphen*)
midterm
midway (*no hyphen*)
MI-5, MI-6 (British intelligence)
MiG (for Russian aircraft designers Mikoyan and
    Gurevich)
Mi'kmaq (*not* Micmac)
mileage (*not* milage; for metric, *use* consumption or
    fuel consumption)
Military Rank—Plurals add "s" to the significant
    rank category, not to the qualifying word.
      —major-generals
      —lieutenant-colonels
      —sergeants major
      —regimental sergeants major
millennium (-nn-), millenniums
Miller, Glenn (band leader, 1904-1944)
Millett, Kate (writer)
millimetre (mm — *sing.* and *pl.* metric symbol, *no
    period*)
mill rate
Milosevic, Slobodan (former Serbian leader)
milquetoast (timid, after comic strip character
    Caspar Milquetoast)
Minamata, Japan
    —Minamata disease
Mini—Hyphenate unless the non-hyphenated form
    is established.

—mini-budget, mini-play, mini-restaurant, mini-sub, but minibike, minibus, minicar, miniseries, miniskirt, minivan

minimum, minimums

minister

—Energy Minister Joe Carney; Joe Carney, energy minister

Minnesota (Minn.)

mint, Royal Canadian Mint, the mint

minus, minuses

minuscule (*not* miniscule)

Minute Rice (trademark for quick-cooking rice)

minutia, minutiae

Miramichi River (N.B.), the Miramichi area

MIRV (for multiple independently targeted re-entry vehicle; always needs explanation)

misinterpret, misinterpreter, misinterpretation

mislead, misled, misleading

Mississauga, Ont.

Mississauga IceDogs

Mississippi (Miss.)

Missouri (Mo.)

Mitchell, Joni (singer)

Mittal Canada Inc. (formerly Ispat Sidbec Inc.)

mixed martial arts

Mixmaster (trademark for food mixer)

MLA (except Ont., Que. and N.L. — member of the legislative assembly) *but avoid*

Mladic, Ratko (Bosnian Serb general)

MNA (Que. — member of national assembly) *but avoid*

Mob (for Mafia), mob (other uses)

moccasin

model, modelled, modelling

Mogadishu

Mohawk (*sing.* and *pl.*)

M

Moldova (formerly Moldavia)

mollusk

Molotov cocktail

Molson Coors Brewing Co. (TSX:TAP.B)
>—Molson Coors Canada Inc. (Canadian
division; TSX:TPX.B)

molybdenum (metallic element and commodity)

Moncton Times and Transcript

money, moneys

money laundering (no hyphen)

monitor

monkey, monkeys

Monroe, Marilyn (1926-1962)

monsieur (*no abbvn.*), messieurs

monsignor, Msgr. Ronald Thom
>—Thom (or the monsignor) said ...

Montana (Mont.)

Monterey, Calif.

Monterrey (Spain, Mexico)

Montgomery, Lucy Maud (1874-1942)

month-long

Months—In dates, abbreviate except March, April,
May, June, July: Jan. 13, 1936; April 2, 1981,
was a Thursday; *but* January 2005, *no commas*.

moon

Moose Jaw Times-Herald

moral (*n.* — lesson, inner meaning; *adj.* — right,
just), moralist, morality

morale (*n.* — mental condition, attitude)

Moral Majority (*no* "the")

Morgentaler, Dr. Henry

Morissette, Alanis (musician)

Moriyama, Raymond (architect)

Mormons (members of the Church of Jesus Christ
of Latter-day Saints)

morocco leather

Morrice, J.W. (painter, 1865-1924)

Morse code

Moslem — *Use* Muslim

mosquito, mosquitoes

Mother's Day (second Sunday in May)

Mother Teresa (1910-1997)

motocross

motto, mottoes

mould (*not* mold)

Mountain—Capitalize when preceding or
    following specific term.
      —Rocky Mountains
      —Mount Edith Cavell (*not* Mt.)

Mountie, Mounties (for RCMP)

Mount Sinai Hospital (Toronto)

Mount Vesuvius

mouse, mousey, mousier

moustache (*not* mus-)

movable (*not* moveable)

moviegoer

Movie Network, the

Mowat, Farley (author)

MP (member of Parliament), MPs (*pl.*), MP's and
    MPs' (*poss.*)

m.p.h. (miles per hour)

MPP (Ontario only — member of the provincial
    parliament) *but avoid*

MP3.com (company)

MP3 player

MRI (for magnetic resonance imaging; *OK in first
    reference*)

Ms. (*period*)

MuchMusic, MuchMoreMusic, MuchMoreRetro

mucous (*adj.* — covered with mucus), mucus (*n.* —
    sticky secretion)

Muhammad (for founder of Islam and all other

M

uses unless user prefers another spelling)

Muhammad Ali

mujahedeen (holy warriors, *pl.*), mujahed (*sing.*)

mukluk (deerskin boot)

mulatto — *Avoid.* Use black-white parentage or some other description.

multi-, multicultural, multilateral, multinational, multimillionaire, multimillion-dollar, multimedia, multiplatform *but* multi-year

Mumbai (formerly Bombay)

—MUMBAI, India (placeline)

mumps (*takes singular verb*)

Murray, Anne (singer)

Muscovite (of Moscow)

muskellunge, muskie

Muskoka (cottage country in Ontario; *not* The Muskokas)

Muslim (*not* Moslem)

must-have (*n., adj.*)

Muzak (trademark for recorded background music)

MV (motor vessel)

Myanmar (formerly Burma, *n.* and *adj.*); Burma can be used in historical references

NAACP (National Association for the
Advancement of Colored People)
NADbank (Newspaper Audience Databank)
naive, naiveté
Namibia (formerly South-West Africa)
Nanaimo Daily News
napa cabbage
naphtha
napoleon (French gold coin, pastry)
NASCAR (*OK in first reference* for National
Association for Stock Car Auto Racing)
Nasdaq
Naskapi, Naskapis
nation, *but uppercase* as part of aboriginal name:
Nisga'a Nation
National, The (CBC news program)
National Action Committee on the Status of
Women (NAC)
National Aeronautics and Space Administration
(NASA *OK in first reference*)
national anthem (*O Canada*)
National Assembly (national legislative body;
Cuban National Assembly) *but* Quebec
national assembly (provincial)
National Capital Region
National Chapter Canada IODE (official name of
Imperial Order of Daughters of the Empire in
Canada)
National Citizens Coalition (*no apostrophe*)
National Defence Headquarters (NDHQ, *but avoid*)
National Energy Board (NEB, *but avoid*)
national energy program
National Farmers Union (NFU, *but avoid*)
National Film Board (NFB)
National Gallery
national government
National Guard (in U.S.)

—a National Guard unit
—a national guardsman
National Hockey League Players' Association
National Library
National Organization for Women (NOW)
National Post, the National Post
National War Memorial (Ottawa)
nationwide (*no hyphen, but prefer* countrywide)
native peoples (includes Indians, Inuit and Métis)
    —native Americans
NATO (North Atlantic Treaty Organization)
Natuashish (Labrador community relocated from
    Davis Inlet)
nautical mile (1.853 kilometres)
Nav Canada
Navy—Capitalize Royal Canadian Navy when
    referring to pre-unification force. For other
    forces, lowercase navy when preceded by the
    name of the country.
    —Royal Canadian Navy until 1968
    —British navy
    —Royal Navy
    —U. S. navy
    —a navy spokesman
    —U.S. 6th Fleet
    —Home Fleet
    —10th Destroyer Flotilla
Nazi (party supporter)
Nazism
NBC (National Broadcasting Co.)
N'djamena (Chad)
Nebraska (Neb.)
Negro, Negroes — *Use* black
neighbour, neighbourhood
Neilson Ltd., William (confectioner)
neoclassical, neoclassicalism

N

Neo-Confucianism
nerve-racking
Netanyahu, Benjamin
Netherlands, the
    —UTRECHT, Netherlands (placeline)
Nevada (Nev.)
New Age (spiritual movement)
New Brunswick (N.B.)
New Brunswick Telegraph-Journal
new Canadian
New Democratic Party (NDP)
New England
newfangled (*one word*)
Newfoundland and Labrador (official name of
    province)
    —N.L. (*abbvn.*)
New Hampshire (N.H.)
New Jersey (N.J.)
newlyweds
New Mexico (N.M.)
news, newsdesk, newsprint, newsroom, newsstand,
    newswire
Newsmaker of the Year (The Canadian Press)
Newsnet (CTV)
Newspaper Guild, the; the guild
Newspaper Names—Lowercase *the* in names
    of newspapers: the Toronto Star; the
    Star; the New York Times, the Times. For
    French-language papers, write Montreal La
    Presse rather than the Montreal La Presse in
    first reference. In subsequent references avoid
    sentence constructions that juxtapose *the* and
    le and *la*:: the La Presse editorial. Alternatives
    include La Presse said in an editorial, an
    editorial in La Presse.
Newsworld (CBC)

N

New Testament
New Westminster, B.C.
New World
New Year's Eve, New Year's Day *but* the new year
(*lowercase*)
New York (N.Y.)
    —New York City
    —New York Thruway
    —New York state
Nexen Inc. (TSX:NXY)
Niagara Escarpment, Peninsula
Niagara-on-the-Lake, Ont.
Nichol, bp (poet, 1944-1988)
Nicholson, Rob (MP)
nickel (coin or metal)
Nickelback (performing group)
Nicknames—Capitalize nicknames generally.
    —the Old Man
    —Reds (for Communists)
    —the Queen City (Regina)
    —the City (London financial area)
    —Iron Curtain
    —Mike (Pinball) Clemons (brackets, not
    quotes); *but* Pinball Clemons (no brackets)
niece
Nielsen Media Research (TV ratings company)
night, guest night, ladies night
nightcap, nightclub, nightdress, nightgown,
    nighthawk, nightlight, nightmare, night owl,
    night school, nightshirt, nighttime, night
    watch
Nike
Nikon (camera)
Nineteen Eighty-Four (George Orwell novel *but* 1984
    for Michael Radford movie)
niqab

Nisga'a, Nisga'a Nation
nitroglycerine
N.L. (abbreviation for Newfoundland and
    Labrador)
    —ST. JOHN'S, N.L.; HAPPY VALLEY-GOOSE
    BAY, N.L. (placelines)
no, noes, no-noes
    —*but* She voted No in the referendum.
Nobel Prize, Nobel Prizes
    —Nobel Peace Prize
    —Nobel Prize in chemistry, physics, etc. but
    Nobel chemistry prize
    —Nobel Memorial Prize in Economic Science
    —Nobel Prize winner, laureate
    —Nobel Prize-winning researcher
    —the prize (*lowercase*)
no man's land
nom de plume, noms de plume
noncommittal
nondescript
non-existent (*not* -ant)
non-fiction (*adj, n.*)
non-life-threatening
nonplus (*v.*), nonplussed
non-profit (*n.* and *adj.*)
non-stick (*adj.*)
no one (*two words*)
Norad (North American Aerospace Defence
    Command)
Nortel Networks Corp. (TSX:NT)
North—Capitalize geographic regions but not their
    derivatives. Lowercase mere direction or
    position.
    —the North (region of Canada)
    —the north (of a province), northern Ontario,
    northern Quebec, etc.

—a northerner
—the northern territories
—northern natives
—Northern Canada
—the Canadian North
—the Far North
—the North Slope (Alaska)
—north of the border
—North-South dialogue
—the northern delegation
—the northern states
—The North defeated the South.
—North Atlantic
—Northern Ireland

North American Aerospace Defence Command
  (Norad *OK in first reference*)
North American Free Trade Agreement (NAFTA)
North Atlantic Treaty Organization (NATO *OK in first reference*)
North Carolina (N.C.)
North Dakota (N.D.)
northeast, northwest (*one word*)
Northern Hemisphere
northern lights
northern Ontario
northern states (of U.S.)
North Pole, the Pole
North Sea
Northwest Atlantic Fisheries Organization (*no abbvn.*)
North West Company
North West Mounted Police
Northwest Passage
Northwest Rebellion (1885)
Northwest Territories (*but* N.W.T.)
  —Northwest Territories council

N

nose, nosy, nosier
nostalgia, nostalgic
noticeable
Notre-Dame Basilica (Montreal)
Nouvelles Télé-Radio (NTR, the French-language
    service of Broadcast News)
Nouvelliste, Le (newspaper in Trois Rivières, Que.)
Nova Chemicals Corp. (*not* NOVA; TSX:NCX)
Nova Scotia (N.S.)
Nova Scotia Power Inc. (*no abbvn.*)
Novocain (trademark for a local anesthetic)
NOW (National Organization for Women)
'N Sync (musical group)
NTR (Nouvelles Télé-Radio)
nucleus, nuclei
number, number 2, No. 2
numskull (*not* numbskull)
Nunassiaq, N.W.T.
Nunatsiavut (region of Labrador controlled by
    Inuit)
Nunavut (Canadian territory, *no abbvn.*)
    —Nunavummiut (resident of Nunavut)
Nuremberg, Germany
Nureyev, Rudolf (ballet, 1938-1993)
nylon

O

Oakland Athletics, Oakland A's
O&Y Properties Corp. (*no periods, no spaces* in O&Y)
oasis, oases
Oath of Allegiance (Canada's official oath)
obbligato
Oberammergau
Obhrai, Deepak (politician)
objet d'art, objets d'art
O Canada
Occidental (race; *avoid*)
occur, occurred, occurrence, occurring
Ocean—Capitalize with specific name.
> —Pacific Ocean
> —the Atlantic and Pacific oceans
> —an ocean wave

October Crisis (1970)
octopus, octopuses
Odd Fellows, Independent Order of (IOOF, *but avoid*), an Odd Fellow
Odesa, Ukraine (*not* Odessa)
odour, odourless *but* odorous
OECD (Organization for Economic Co-operation and Development)
Oedipus
off, offbeat, off-centre, off-duty, off-line, off-season, offshore, offside, offstage, off-white; blastoff (*n.*), blast off (*v.*).
> Similarly: cutoff, layoff, payoff, playoff, sendoff, standoff, stopoff, takeoff (all *n.*)

offence, offensive
office, county clerk's office
> —Home Office (U.K.)
> —Foreign Office (U.K.)

officer cadet (*no abbvn.*)
> —Officer Cadet Andrew Glenny

officer of the Order of the British Empire (OBE)

O

officers mess
O'Hara, Catherine (actor)
Ohio (*no abbvn.*)
oilfield, oilpatch, oilsands (*one word*)
Ojibwa (Indian — rhymes with way) (*sing.* and *pl.*)
OK (*not* OK!) magazine
OK (*not* okay), OK'd, OK'ing
Okalik, Paul (first premier of Nunavut)
Oklahoma (*not* Oklahoma!) musical
Oklahoma (Okla.)
Oktoberfest (beer-drinking festival)
old age pension
Old Boys club, network
old-fashioned
Old Testament
old-time, old-timer
Olivier, Laurence (1907-1989)
Olympic Games, the Games
    —the Winter Olympics, the Olympics, the
    Summer Games
    —flag-bearer, medallist
ombudsman, ombudsmen
    —ombudsman Jill Leonard
omelette
Ondaatje, Michael
One-Eleven (British aircraft)
one-time (*adj., hyphen for all uses*)
Onex Corp. (TSX:OCX)
online (all uses)
onstage, offstage
Ontario (Ont.), Ontarian
Ontario Health Insurance Plan (OHIP, *but avoid*)
Ontario Lottery and Gaming Corp. (*not*
    Corporation; OLG OK *in second reference*)
Ontario Power Generation (formerly Ontario
    Hydro)

O

Ontario Provincial Police (*but* the provincial police)
Ontario Teachers' Pension Plan, Teachers' (*second reference*)
onto (*prep.*)
OPEC (Organization of Petroleum Exporting Countries)
ophthalmologist, ophthalmology
Opposition—Capitalize when referring to the official Opposition. Otherwise, lowercase.
    —an opposition viewpoint, sat in opposition
    —the Opposition leader
opus, opuses
Orange Crush (trademark for pop)
orbit (*n.* and *v.*), orbital, orbiting
order-in-council, orders-in-council
Order of Canada
    —companion of the Order of Canada (recipients may use initials CC)
    —officer of the order (initials OC)
    —member of the order (initials CM)
ordinary seaman (*no abbvn.*)
    —Ordinary Seaman Alain Delisle
Oregon (Ore.)
Organization for Economic Co-operation and Development (OECD)
Organization for Security and Co-operation in Europe
Organization of African Unity (OAU)
Organization of American States (OAS)
Organization of Petroleum Exporting Countries (OPEC)
organize
Orient, Oriental (race; *but use* Asia, Asian)
    —an oriental flavour
    —Orient Express (train)
Orillia Packet and Times

O

orneriness, ornery
ornithology
orthopedic
Osbourne, Ozzy
Osgoode Hall (home of Ontario Appeal Court)
Otello (Verdi and Rossini operas), Othello
      (Shakespeare play)
Ottawa Renegades (CFL team)
Ottawa Rough Riders (former CFL team)
Ottawa 67's (hockey team)
Ouellet, André
out, outbid, outboard, outbox, outfield, outpatient,
      outtake (film); fadeout (*n.*), fade out (*v.*).
      Similarly: fallout, hideout, pullout, shootout,
      shutout, takeout, walkout (all *n.*)
Outaouais, western Quebec
OUTtv
Oval Office
overall, overalls (garment)
overall (all-embracing)
Owen Sound Sun Times
Oxfam Canada
oxford (cloth, shoe)
Ozawa, Seiji (conductor)
ozone

P

Pablum (trademark for a baby cereal), *but* pabulum (food)

pact, Baghdad Pact, Warsaw Pact

page 2, pages 1-3; p. 2, pp. 1-3 (*abbvn.* for tabulation)

Pahlavi, Mohammad Reza (shah, 1919-1980)

paleontologist, paleontology

Palestine Liberation Organization (PLO)

pallbearer (*one word*)

Palm Pilot

panacea

Panama, Isthmus of

Panama Canal

panama hat

Pan American Games, Pan Am Games (*no hyphen*)

panda (*not* panda bear)

panel, panellist, panelling

pantyhose

paparazzi (*pl.*), paparazzo (*sing.*)

paper-boy, paper-clip, paper-girl

Pap smear, test

Papua New Guinea (*no hyphen*)

paraffin (wax; in Britain, kerosene)

paragraph 2

parallel, paralleled, 49th parallel

Paralympics

paralyze (*not* -se), paralysis

paranoia, paranoiac, paranoid

paraphernalia (*pl.*)

paraplegic

parenthesis, parentheses

parimutuel (*no hyphen*)

Parisien Libéré (newspaper — *not* Libre)

park, Banff National Park, High Park

Parker Bowles, Camilla (*now* Duchess of Cornwall)

Parkinson's disease, Parkinsonism

Parks Canada
Parliament, member of (MP, MPs)
parliament
   —Parliament (national legislature)
   —parliament (provincial or regional)
   —parliamentary
   —Parliament Buildings (Ottawa)
   —Israel's parliament, the Knesset
parlour
Parmesan cheese
   —Parmigiano-Reggiano
parole, paroled, parolee
ParticipAction
partier, partygoer
Parti indépendantiste
Parti Québécois (PQ), Québécois's (*poss.*)
   —Péquiste (*n., adj.*)
partisan
part time, a part-time job, a part-timer
party, Communist party, Green party, Liberal party
   —*but* New Democratic Party (NDP)
   —Parti Québécois (PQ)
Pashto (language in Afghanistan and Pakistan)
Passchendaele
passerby, passersby
pasteurize, pasteurizing
pastime
patchwork (*one word*)
Patriot (U.S. missile)
Pavarotti, Luciano
pavilion (*not* pavillion)
paycheque (*one word*)
payday (*one word*)
pay off (*v.*), payoff (*n.*)
payola
payroll (*no hyphen*)

P

pay TV, pay TV network (*no hyphen*)
PC (*OK in first reference* for personal computer)
PCB (polychlorinated biphenyl), PCBs
PDA (personal digital assistant)
pea, peameal bacon, pea soup, pea-soup fog,
     pea-souper (fog)
Peace Corps (U.S.)
peacekeeping
peacemaker
peacetime
peak (mountain, apex); peek (peer)
peccadillo, peccadillos
pedagogy
pedal (bicycle), pedaller, pedalling
peddle (to sell), pedlar (seller), peddling, softpedal
     (*not* -peddle)
pediatrician
pedlar (seller)
pedophile
peewee
Peggy's Cove, N.S.
pekinese (dog)
pemmican (dried meat)
Penetanguishene, Ont.
penicillin
penitentiary, Kingston Penitentiary
Pennsylvania (Pa.)
pension, Canada Pension Plan (CPP, *but avoid*)
Pepsi, Pepsi-Cola (trademarks for a cola drink)
pep talk (*two words*)
Péquiste
perceive, perceived, perceiving
per cent, percentage, six per cent increase (*no
     hyphens*)
perennial
perestroika

perfunctory
perimeter (*not* -re)
periphery
permafrost (*no hyphen*)
permissible (*not* -able)
perogy, perogies
perquisite (perk), prerequisite (requirement)
Perrier (trademark for a mineral water)
perseverance, persevere, persevering
Pershing, Pershing 2 missile
Persian Gulf (*not* Arabian Gulf)
    —Persian Gulf War
persian lamb
persistence (*not* -ance), persistency, persistent (*not* -ant)
persona non grata
persuade, persuadable, persuasible, persuasion, persuasive
Petro-Canada (*hyphen; no abbvn.;* TSX:PCA)
petrochemical (*no hyphen*)
petty officer (*no abbvn.*)
    —chief petty officer (first class) (*no abbvn.*)
    —petty officer (first class) (*no abbvn.*)
PGA (Professional Golfers Association)
Phalange party (Lebanon)
pharaoh
phase, Phase 1 (*not* phase one)
PhD (doctor of philosophy)
phenomenon, phenomena
Philadelphia Inquirer (newspaper)
Philadelphia 76ers (*no apostrophe*)
Philip (usual spelling of first name)
    —Prince Philip
Philippe
Philippines, the
    —QUEZON CITY, Philippines (placeline)

P

—Filipinos (the people)
philistine (lowercase for someone lacking culture)
Phnom Penh, Cambodia
Phoebe
phoney (*not* phony), phoneys
phosphorus (*not* -ous)
photo-engraver, photo-engraving
phys-ed
piastre (*not* -er)
Picchio Pharma Inc.
piccolo, piccolos
picket (*not* picketer), picketed, picketing
pick up (*v.*), pickup (*n.* or *adj.*)
picnic, picnicker
piecemeal
pigeonhole (*no hyphen*)
pileup (*n.*)
pill (*lowercase* for birth control pill, the pill)
pilot officer (*no abbvn.*)
PIN (personal identification number)
pinch-hitter
Pinot Noir, Blanc (wine)
pin up (*v.*), pin-up (*n.*)
pipeline
    —*but* TransCanada PipeLines Ltd.
pixel, pixelate (divide into pixels)
pizzazz
placeline
    —CORNER BROOK, N.L.
    —MacGREGOR, Man. (for MacGregor)
    —MACKENZIE, B.C. (for Mackenzie)
plagiarism, plagiarize
plainclothes police
    —police in plain clothes
plan, Colombo Plan, Marshall Plan
plaster of paris

plateau, plateaus

platoon sergeant (Platoon Sgt.)

platypus, platypuses

play off (*v.*), playoff (*n.*)

PlayStation

 —PSP (PlayStation Portable)

playwright, *but* playwriting

PLC (public limited company)

pleaded (*preferred to* pled for past tense of plead)

Plexiglas (trademark for an acrylic plastic)

PLO (Palestine Liberation Organization)

plow (*not* plough)

plummet, plummeted

plus, pluses

p.m., a.m.

podcast

pogey (slang for employment insurance)

poinsettia

Point Lepreau

Polanyi, John (Nobel Prize in chemistry, 1986)

Polaroid (trademark for camera, sunglasses)

Pole, the; North Pole, South Pole

Police—Uppercase when using the formal name of
 a force. Otherwise, lowercase.

 —provincial police, regional police

 —Toronto Police Service, *but* a Toronto police
 officer, Toronto police

 —Ontario Provincial Police (OPP)

 —*but* Quebec provincial police (*no abbvn.*)

 —Royal Canadian Mounted Police (RCMP)

 —Mounties (for RCMP)

 —police chief

 —police Chief Arnold Goldberg, Deputy
 Chief Emma Vokey

 —police commission

 —Quebec police commission

—police court, station

policy-maker

polio (short for poliomyelitis)

Politburo

Politics—Capitalize political parties, as Liberal,
Labour, Socialist, *but* lowercase the words
when referring to philosophical attitudes.
Capitalize Opposition when referring to the
official Opposition, the non-governing party
with the most seats.

polka-dot (*hyphen*)

Pollyanna

polygamist (*n.*) polygamous (*adj.*)

pompom

Ponteix, Sask.

pontiff (for Pope)

pope, Pope Benedict, the Pope (current pontiff),
former pope, popes of history

poppyseed (*n.* and *adj.*)

Popsicle (trademark for ice on a stick)

pore (*v.* — study earnestly), pored, poring

Porsche

Portage la Prairie, Man.

Port aux Basques, N.L.

porterhouse steak

portland cement

Portuguese

postdate (*v.*), postdated cheque

postelection

post-game

postgraduate

Post-it notes (trademark)

postmaster general, postmasters general

post-mortem (*hyphen*)

post-season (*hyphen*)

post-secondary

postwar

potato, potatoes

potlatch (aboriginal gift, ceremony)

potshot

poutine

PoW (prisoner of war), PoWs

Power Corp.

power of attorney (*no hyphens*)

powwow (*n.* and *v.*)

PR (for public relations)

practicable (can be done), practical (useful, functional)

practice (*n.* or *adj.*), practise (*v.*)

prairie
   —Prairie provinces
   —the Prairies
   —their Prairie farm
   —the prairie was parched in drought

pre, prearrange, Precambrian shield, pre-Christian, precondition, predate, pre-election,

precede, precedence (priority)

precedent (earlier instance)

pre-empt, preheat, premarital, preoccupy, prepaid, preschool, preschooler, pre-season, pre-tax, preteen, prewar

prefer, preferable, preferably, preference (*not* -ance), preferential, preferred

Premier—Use for Canadian provinces and territories, Australian states, France and former French colonies.
   —Premier Ann Bostwick
   —deputy premier Henry Miller (informal position)
   —premiers conference
   —former premier Roy Romanow
   —the premier of Ontario

première (*n.* and *v.*)

—*but* a premier attraction
prerequisite (requirement), perquisite (perk)
prerogative (*not* perog-)
Presbyterian Church in Canada
president, President Barack Obama
> —the president said ...
> —former president George W. Bush
> —president-elect Barack Obama
> —Treasury Board President Vic Toews
> —Toyota Canada president Yoichi Tomihara

Presidents Day (U.S.)
Presque Isle, Me.
Presqu'ile Point, Ont.
Presse, La (Montreal newspaper)
Presse Canadienne, La (PC)
press gallery
> —Parliamentary Press Gallery Association
> —press gallery dinner
> —worked in the press gallery

pretence
prevalence, prevalent
prevent, preventable, preventer (*not* -or), preventive
(*not* preventative)
price tag (*two words*)
PricewaterhouseCoopers
pricey
Priestley, Jason (actor)
Primakov, Yevgeny (Russia)
prime time, prime-time program
prince
> —Prince Charles, Charles, the prince; Charles,
> Prince of Wales; the Prince of Wales
> —Crown Prince Abdullah

Prince Edward Island, the Island (P.E.I.)
princess

—Princess Anne, Anne, the princess
—*but* the Princess of Wales or Diana (*not* Princess Diana)

Princess Patricia's Canadian Light Infantry

principal (main, most important), school principal
—school principal Paul Chambers

principle (fundamental belief)

prison (use for federal institutions, not holding cells or provincial jails)
—Oakalla prison farm

prisoner of war (PoW, PoWs)

private (Pte. Bob Lively)
—private first class (Pte. 1st Class)

private member's bill

privatize, privatization

privilege

Privy Council (*uppercase*)
—Privy Council Office (*no abbvn.*)

proactive

processor

Procter & Gamble Co., P&G (*OK in second reference*), P&G Canada

prodigy, prodigies, prodigious

professor, Prof. Normand Saint-Onge

program (*not* -mme), programmer, programming
—national energy program

Prohibition (alcohol outlawed)

Promised Land

promulgate, promulgation, promulgator (*not* -er)

proofread

propaganda

propellant (*n.*), propellent (*adj.*)

propeller (*not* -or)

prophecy (*n.*), prophesy (*v.*)

Prophet, the (Muhammad in Islam)

prorogue

P

prospectus, prospectuses
prostate (male gland); prostrate (lying face down; overcome)
Protestant, Protestantism (religion)
protester (*not* -or)
province, provincial
      —province of Ontario (geography)
      —Province of Ontario bonds (corporation)
provincewide
proviso, provisos
p's and q's
psychedelic
psychiatric, psychiatrist, psychiatry
psychic
psychopath, psychopathic
psychosis, psychoses
psychosomatic
publicly (*never* publically)
Pulitzer Prize
      —a Pulitzer Prize-winning writer
pulley, pulleys
pulp mill (*two words*)
Punxsutawney, Pa.
Pusan — *Use* Busan for city in South Korea
Pushkin, Alexander
push over (*v.*), pushover (*n.*)
push up (*v.*), pushup (*n.*)
Putin, Vladimir
putt (golf)
Pygmy
pyjamas
Pyrex (trademark for heat-resistant cookware)

Q

Qantas Airways
Qatar
Q-Tips (trademark for cotton swabs on a stick)
quadriplegic
Quai d'Orsay (French Foreign Ministry)
Quakers (Society of Friends)
quandary
Qu'Appelle, Sask.
quarter-final *but* semifinal
quarter-horse
quartet
quarto, quartos
Quebec (Que.), Quebecer (*not* -ck)
Quebec City (*but* Quebec in placelines)
Québécois, Parti Québécois (PQ)
Quebecor Inc. (TSX:QBR.B)
Quebec provincial police (*lowercase, no abbvn.*)
Queen Elizabeth 2 (liner), QE2
Queen Mother (Elizabeth, 1900-2002)
Queen's counsel (QC)
Queen's Park
Queen's Plate
Queen's University, Kingston, Ont.
question-and-answer, Q-and-A, Q-and-A's
questionnaire
question period (*lowercase*)
quiche Lorraine
quixotic (extravagantly chivalrous; from Don
      Quixote)
Quonset (hut)
Quotidien, Le (newspaper in Chicoutimi, Que.)
Qur'an (*not* Koran)

R

rabbi, Rabbi Stuart Rosenberg

raccoon, raccoons

race, race card, racecourse, racehorse, racetrack,
    raceway

racked (their brains)

racket (bat used in tennis, badminton, etc.)

racquetball (game)

Radio, Television Stations—Use this style: CFCF
    Montreal, CHUM-FM Toronto, CBC-TV. If a
    station uses another name, follow its style:
    Mix 99.9, 680News

Radio-Canada (*hyphen*)

Radio Moscow (*but* Moscow radio)

radius, radii

railway (*preferred to* railroad)
    —*but* Long Island Rail Road

railworker

rain, raindrop, rainfall, rainforest, rainstorm

RAM (random access memory)

Ramadan

rancour *but* rancorous

Rand (*not* RAND) Worldwide

R&B (rhythm and blues)

Ranger 4 (satellite)

rapt (absorbed, intent)

rarefy, rarefied

rational (sensible)

rationale (statement of reasons)

Ratzinger, Joseph (Pope Benedict XVI)

raucous (*not* -cus)

rayon

razzmatazz (*no hyphens*)

RBC Financial Group (TSX:RY)
    —RBC or Royal Bank (Canadian banking
    arm)

re-, readmit, reassess, recur, recurrence, re-examine,

re-enter, reinstate, reissue, reopen, reorganize, re-cover (cover again), recover (regain), re-lay (lay again), relay (pass on), reroute, rerun, re-sign (sign again), resign (quit), reunite, reuse, reusable

Reader's Digest (*not* Readers')

ready-made (*hyphen*)

reality, realization, realize (*not* -ise)

Realtor—In Canada, a trademark and must be capitalized. Not a synonym for real estate agent. It identifies members of the Canadian Real Estate Association and the (U.S.) National Association of Realtors, which includes agents or brokers, *but* also property managers, developers and other real estate professionals.

REAL Women

rearguard

rebut, refute (prove wrong; *use with care*)

recoilless

Red (Communist, *but avoid*)

Red Cross, Red Cross Society, Red Crescent
—a Red Cross campaign

redneck (rustic, poor white)

Reeves, Keanu

refer, referred

referendum, referendums

Reformation

reformatory, Guelph reformatory

refuel, refuelled

refute, rebut (prove wrong; *use with care*)

reggae

regiment, 24th Regiment

regimental sergeant major (Regimental Sgt. Maj.)
—regimental sergeants major (*no abbvn.*)

Regina Leader-Post

R

region, Peel Region
registered education savings plan (RESP)
registered retirement savings plan (RRSP)
reign (rule), rein (leather strap, symbol of power)
Religion—Capitalize names of religions and
denominations.
—American Lutheran Church
—Anglican Church of Canada
—Baha'i faith
—Buddhism, Buddhist
—Church of Christ, Scientist (also Christian
Science Church)
—Church of Jesus Christ of Latter-day Saints
—Greek Orthodox Church
—Hinduism, Hindu
—Islam, Muslim
—Jehovah's Witnesses
—Judaism (Orthodox, Reform, Conservative)
—Pentecostal Assembly
—Presbyterian Church in Canada
—Roman Catholic Church
—Seventh-day Adventist
—Ukrainian Orthodox Church
—United Church of Canada
relinquish
R.E.M. (musical group)
Remembrance Day (Nov. 11)
reminiscent
removable (*not* -eable)
remuneration
Renaissance (historic period), a renaissance of
painting (general sense)
rendezvous (*n.* and *v.*)
renowned
repechage (rowing)
repel, repellent

repent, repentance, repentant
repertoire, repertory
representative (U.S. Congress)
    —Rep. Donna Hooper
    —Rep. Robert Brown
reprieve
republic, Fifth Republic
    —Republic of Ireland
    —the Irish republic
Republican (party or member)
    —Republican party (U.S.)
republican (philosophical attitude)
requiem, requiem mass
research and development, R&D (*no periods*)
reserve (*preferred to* reservation for aboriginal lands
    in Canada), the Chippewa reserve
re-sign (sign again), resign (quit)
resistance, resistibility, resistible (*not* -able)
respectability, respectable
restaurateur (*not* restauranteur)
resumé
resuscitate
retired, retired brigadier Pat Turner
Reuters, Reuters news agency
reverend
    —Rev. Alan Cross (Protestant and RC; Cross
    on second reference)
reverse, reversible
revolution, American Revolution
revolutions per minute (r.p.m.)
Reye's syndrome
Rh (for Rhesus) factor, Rh positive, Rh negative
rhinoceros (*sing.* and *pl.*)
Rhode Island (R.I.)
Rhodes Scholar, Scholarship
rhododendron

R

Rice, Condoleezza
Richler, Mordecai (author, 1931-2001)
Richter scale
Richthofen, Baron von (Red Baron, 1892-1918)
ricochet, ricocheted
Rideau Hall
rifleman (*no abbvn.*)
    —Rifleman Andrew Coates
right, right field, right-fielder, right wing,
right-handed, right-hander (*hyphen*)
right-winger; right-field wall, right-handed pitcher,
    right-wing politician (*adj., hyphen*)
rigor mortis
rigour *but* rigorous
ringtone *(one word)*
Rio de Janeiro
Rio Tinto Alcan
rip off (*v.*), ripoff (*n.*)
river, St. Lawrence River
Riyadh
RJR-Macdonald Inc. — now JTI-Macdonald Corp.
Road—Capitalize when used with names,
    abbreviate in numbered street addresses.
       —along Kingston Road
       —10 Scott Rd. E.
roadblock (*one word*), road map (*two words*)
Rock, the (informal for Newfoundland or Gibraltar)
Rockefeller Center
rock 'n' roll
rococo
Rodrigue (given name — *not* -que)
Rogers Centre, Toronto (formerly SkyDome)
Rogers Communications Inc. (TSX:RCI.B)
       —Rogers Cable
       —Rogers Media
       —Rogers Video

—Rogers Wireless
Rogers Pass, B.C.
rollcall (*one word*)
Rollerblades (trademark for in-line skates),
  Rollerblading (*but use* in-line skating)
roller-coaster, roller derby, roller-skate (*v.*), roller
  skates
rollover (*n.*)
Rolls-Royce Ltd., a Rolls-Royce
Rolodex
roly-poly (*hyphen*)
ROM (read only memory)
Roma (*preferred to* Gypsy)
Roman Catholic (Roman may be dropped only if
  reference is obvious)
Romanesque
Romania (*not* Rumania)
roman numerals, type
Roman Numerals—Use roman numerals to
  indicate sequence for people and animals and
  in proper names where specified. Otherwise
  prefer arabic numerals as easier to grasp.
  —Pope Benedict XVI, Henry VIII, *The
  Godfather, Part II*
roof, roofs
room, Room 4, Oak Room
  —in the assembly room
Rorschach test
Rosh Hashanah
Rothmans Inc. (TSX:ROC)
Rothschild
Rottweiler
roundtable (*one word, n. and adj.*)
roundup (*n.*), round up (*v.*)
Royal Air Force (Britain)
royal assent

R

Royal Canadian Air Force (until 1968)
Royal Canadian Legion
     —the legion announced ...
     —parade of legionnaires
Royal Canadian Mint, the mint
Royal Canadian Mounted Police (RCMP)
     —RCMP musical ride
     —the Mounties
Royal Canadian Navy (until 1968)
Royal Family (British), royal family (other nations)
Royal Ontario Museum (ROM, *but avoid*)
royal tour, visit
royalty
Roy Thomson Hall (Toronto)
r.p.m. (revolutions per minute)
RRSP (registered retirement savings plan)
RSS (*OK in first reference* for Really Simple
     Syndication)
ruble
Rugby—centre, fly half, fullback, lineout, scrum
     half, Test match, try, tries
rumour
runner-up, runners-up
run-off, run-up
rural route
     —RR 2, Newmarket
rush hour, rush-hour traffic
Russia
RV (for recreational vehicle)
Rwanda
Ryerson University (Toronto)

S

'**S**—To denote the possessive add 's to singular and plural nouns not ending in "s": mother's purse, women's shoes, alumni's gifts. Add it to singular nouns ending in "s" to indicate a sis or siz sound: the boss's secretary, Strauss's waltzes, Duplessis's cabinet. But names ending with an -iz sound and classical names ending in "s" often take the apostrophe only: Bridges' ideas, Socrates' plays.

Sabbath

saccharin (*n.*), saccharine (*adj.*)

sacrilegious

Saddam Hussein (1937-2006); Saddam *in second reference*

Sadler's Wells Ballet

Sailboats—Capitalize names of classes of racing and pleasure craft.

—Tornado, International Europe

Sainte-Marie, Buffy (singer-composer)

Sainte-Marie among the Hurons (Midland, Ont.)

Saint John, N.B.

Saint Mary's University (Halifax)

salability, salable (*not* -eable)

Salchow, triple Salchow (figure-skating jump)

salmonella

SALT (for strategic arms limitation talks)

Salvadoran

Salvation Army, the Army, a Salvationist

salvo, salvos (*pl.*)

SAM (for surface-to-air missile)

Samaritan, Good

Sanaa, Yemen

sanatorium, sanatoriums

sanctimonious

Sanforized (trademark for material that won't shrink)

S

San Francisco 49ers (*no apostrophe*)
Sanka (trademark for a decaffeinated coffee)
sapper (*no abbvn.*)
    —Sapper John Flynn
Sarajevo
Saran Wrap (trademark for a plastic film)
SARS (severe acute respiratory syndrome, *OK in first reference*)
Saskatchewan (*not* Regina) Roughriders (*one word*)
Saskatchewan (Sask.)
Saskatchewan Party
    —Sask. Party *OK if abbreviation needed*
saskatoon (berry)
Saskatoon StarPhoenix
sasquatch (mysterious ape-like creature)
Satan, satanic, Satanism
Sault Ste. Marie, Ont. and Mich.
    —the Sault (*not* the Soo)
    —*but* Soo Greyhounds hockey team
    —the Sault Star
Savile Row (London)
saviour, Saviour (Christ)
savory (herb)
savour, savoury (flavour)
saxophone
scare, scary, scarier
scarf, scarves
scarlet fever
Scene 2, the second scene
sceptic — *Use* skeptic
Schafer, R. Murray (composer)
Schefferville, Que.
schizophrenia, schizophrenic
scholar, Rhodes Scholar, Scholarship
School—Capitalize when using proper name.
    —Leaside High School

—Our Lady of Sorrows School
—London School of Economics
—University of Toronto Schools
—Royal York Academy *(proper name)* but
Royal York high school
—Kingslake Public School *(proper name)* but
Kingslake elementary school
—the McGill medical school
—day school, private school
—Sunday school
—school board, schoolbook, schoolboy, school
bus, schoolchildren, schoolgirl, school guard,
school teacher, school trustee, schoolyard
Schumann, Robert (composer, 1810-1856)
Schwarzenegger, Arnold
Scorsese, Martin (film director)
Scotch Tape (trademark for sticky tape)
Scotch whisky
Scotiabank, Scotiabank Group (TSX:BNS)
—Bank of Nova Scotia (legal name)
—ScotiaMcLeod (retail brokerage)
—Scotia Capital Inc. (corporate investment
arm)
Scotsman *(not Scotchman)*
Scots or Scottish *(not Scotch)*
scout
—Scouts Canada
—the Scouts (association)
—a scout
—eagle scout (U.S.)
—Beaver
—Cub
—Chief Scout's Award
—Venturer Scout, Venturers
Scrabble (trademark for a word game)
Screech (rum)

Scripture (Bible)

S-curve

scuttlebutt (*no hyphen*)

Sea—Capitalize when preceding or following the
    specific term.
    —Sea of Galilee
    —Black Sea

Sea-Doo (trademark for a brand of personal
    watercraft)

Seafarers International Union of Canada (SIU)

SEAL (U.S. navy)

seaman
    —able seaman (*no abbvn.*)
    —leading seaman (*no abbvn.*)
    —ordinary seaman (*no abbvn.*)

Sears Canada Inc. (TSX:SCC)
    —a Sears store, Sears

Seasons—Lowercase for spring, summer, fall or
    autumn, winter

season's greetings

seatbelt (*one word*)

SEATO (for Southeast Asia Treaty Organization)

seaway, St. Lawrence Seaway
    —St. Lawrence Seaway Authority
    —St. Lawrence Seaway Development Corp.

second lieutenant (2nd Lieut. Marie Demers)

Second World War (*not* World War II)

secretary general (*no hyphen*)

Section 23, Sec. 5

Security Council (UN)

seder

Seeing Eye (trademark for guide dog)

seigneur, seigniory

semi, semi-annual, semi-automatic, semicircle,
    semicolon, semifinal (*but* quarter-final),
    semifinalist, semi-invalid, semi-official,

semitransparent, semitropical, semi-weekly
Semite, Semitism, anti-Semitism
Senate (national legislature); senate (state
    legislature)
    —the university senate
senator (Canada and U.S.)
    —Sen. Edward Kennedy, Sen. Nancy Greene
    —former senator Robert de Cotret
senior chief petty officer (*no abbvn.*)
sensual (gratifying to the body, especially sexually),
    sensuous (appealing to the senses, especially
    through beauty)
separate school, school board
Sept. 11 (day of terrorist attacks in United States;
    not September 11), 9-11
Serb (*n.*), Serbian (*adj.*)
Serbia and Montenegro (formerly Yugoslavia)
    —SERBIA-MONTENEGRO (placelines)
sergeant (Sgt. Margaret Bonotto)
    —staff sergeant (Staff Sgt. Margaret Bonotto)
sergeant-at-arms
sergeant first class (Sgt. 1st Class)
sergeant major (Sgt. Maj. Fred Tylee)
    —regimental sergeant major (Regimental Sgt.
    Maj.)
    —sergeants major (*pl.*)
series (*generally lowercase*)
    —*but* World Series, the Series, Little League
    World Series
set up (*v.*), setup (*n.*)
Seventh-day Adventist
7Up (soft drink)
    —Seven-Up (corporate references)
severe acute respiratory syndrome (SARS *OK in*
    first reference)
sewage (waste), sewerage (drainage)

S

Sex and the City (TV show, *not Sex in the City*)
sextet
sexually transmitted disease (STD *but avoid*)
Shaffer, Paul (bandleader)
shakable (*not* -eable)
shake down (*v.*), shakedown (*n. and adj.*)
shake out (v.), shakeout (*n. and adj.*)
Shakespeare, Shakespearean
shake up (*v.*), shakeup (*n.*)
shaky, shakier, shakiness
shalom (greeting)
shaman, shamans (*pl.*), Shamanism
shanghai (*v.*), shanghaied, shanghaiing
Shangri-La
shanty, shanties
Sharansky, Natan
Shariah (Muslim code of religious law)
Shaw Communications Inc. (TSX:SJR.B)
sheik (*not* shiek)
shellac, shellacking
shemozzle (commotion)
sheriff, Sheriff Anton Gerber
Sheshatshiu, Labrador (formerly Sheshatsheit)
Shiite Muslim
Shippagan, N.B. (*not* Shippegan)
shipwreck (*no hyphen*)
Shirleys Bay, Ont. (*no apostrophe*)
shish kebab
shiva
shivaree (friendly invasion of newlyweds' home)
shlemiel (foolish, unlucky person)
shlep (to drag)
shlock (shoddy)
shmaltz (sentimentality)
shmo (a fool, a clumsy person)
shmooz (chat)

shnook (a patsy)
shnorrer (a moocher, panhandler)
shoo-in
shoot out (*v.*), shootout (*n.*)
Shoppers Drug Mart Corp. (TSX:SC)
shoptalk
short list (*n.*) shortlist (*v.*)
shortwave (broadcasting)
shotgun (*one word*)
shot put (*two words*)
show, flower show, horse show
shtick (a gimmick; clowning)
shut out (*v.*), shutout (*n.*)
siamese twins (*use* joined twins or description:
        babies born attached at the hips)
side-effect
Sidney, B.C.
SIDS (*but use* sudden infant death syndrome *in first
        reference*)
siege (*not* -ei-)
sight, sightseeing, sightseer
signal, signalled, signaller
signalman (no abbvn.)
        —Signalman William O'Callaghan
Sikh, the Sikh religion
Siksika (aboriginal band)
silhouette
Silicon Valley
silo, silos
Simoniz (trademark for a car wax)
Sinn Fein
sinus, sinuses
siphon (*not* syphon)
sir, Sir John Jones; Sir John *or preferably* Jones *in
        second reference*
sirocco (Italian name for Sahara wind)

sitcom (TV situation comedy)

sizable (*not* -eable)

skating, figure skating, ice skating, speed skating
   (*hyphenate when used adjectivally*)

skeptic, skeptical, skepticism (*not* sc-)

ski, skier, skis, skiing

Ski-Doo (snowmobile trademark)

skid row (*not* road)

skilful

skulduggery

slaughterhouse

Slovakia

small-c conservative

smallmouth (bass)

Smallwood, Joey (*not* Joseph, 1900-1991)

smart-alec

smartphone (*one word*)

Smiths Falls, Ont. (*no apostrophe*)

Smithsonian Institution (*not* Institute)

smoky (*not* smokey)

smorgasbord

smoulder

SMS (for short message service. *Prefer* text message)

snakehead (human smuggler)

SNC-Lavalin Group Inc. (TSX:SNC)

snob, snobbery, snobbish, snobbishness

snow, snowblower, snowboard, snowfall,
   snowflake, snowflurries, snowstorm

snowbirds (Canadians who winter in the South)

Snowbirds (Canadian Forces flying team)

snowboard cross (*two words*)

snowmobile (*one word*)

snowshoe, snowshoer

s.o.b.

sober

Sobeys Inc., a Sobeys store

Social Crediter (*not* -or)
Social Credit party
socialism, socialist (philosophical attitude)
Socialist (party or member)
Société franco-manitobaine, la
society, Audubon Society
Socred (*n.* and *adj.*)
softpedal (*not* -peddle)
soft-spoken (*hyphen*)
software
softy, softies
Soleil, Le (Quebec)
solicitor general, solicitors general
solo, solos
soluble
Solzhenitsyn, Alexander
Somali (*n.*), Somalian (*adj.*)
sombre (*not* -er)
some, someday, someplace, somebody, somebodies,
    somehow, someone, something, at some time
    (*two words*), sometime (*adv.; adj.*), somewhat,
    somewhere
Somers, Harry (composer, 1925-99)
somersault
soprano, sopranos
SOS (*no periods*)
Sotheby's Canada Inc.
    —Sotheby's for short
South Asia, South Asian (*not* East India, East
    Indian)
South Carolina (S.C.)
South Dakota (S.D.)
southeast (*one word*)
    —Southeast Asia (region), southeast Asian
    (*adj.*)
    —Southeast Asia Treaty Organization

(SEATO)

Southern Canada, southern Canadian weather

southern France

Southern Hemisphere

southern Ontario

southern states (U.S.)

South Pole, the Pole

sou'wester (waterproof hat)

sovereigntist (*not* sovereignist)

sovereignty-association

Soviet Union, former (Union of Soviet Socialist
Republics, U.S.S.R.)

soybean, soy sauce

spacewalk

spam (Internet)

Spanish Civil War

spartan

Speaker—Capitalize in all references to avoid
ambiguity.
—Speaker Martha Lim, the Speaker
—deputy Speaker Glenn Eckert, the deputy
Speaker, former Speaker

Special Investigations Unit (SIU - Ontario)

spectre (*not* -er)

speech from the throne

speedskater, speedskating

spellbinder (*no hyphen*)

spellcheck, spellchecker (*one word*)

Sphinx (representation near pyramids)

sphinx (winged monster)

Spider-Man (comic, movie)

Spielberg, Steven

spina bifida

spin off (*v.*), spinoff (*n.* and *adj.*)

splendour

spoonful, spoonfuls

sports writer *(two words)*
sport utility vehicle (*not* sports; SUV)
spring (season)
squadron leader (*no abbvn.*)
Squid-Jiggin' Ground, the (Newfoundland ballad)
Srebrenica (Bosnia)
Sri Lanka, Sri Lankan
 —Sri Lanka Freedom party
SS (Schutzstaffel, Nazi elite guard)
SS (steamship)
St-, Ste-, St.—Use abbreviations in federal and
 provincial names of political ridings. Use St.
 for male and female saints: St. Peter, St. Anne.
stadium, stadiums
staff, staffs (poles), staves (music)
staff inspector, Staff Insp. Albert Dupont
staff sergeant (Staff Sgt.)
Stalin, Josef (1879-1953)
stampede, Calgary Stampede, the Stampede
Standard & Poor's Corp.
 —S&P/TSX composite index
standardbred, thoroughbred
standard time
 —eastern, central, mountain standard time
 —Atlantic, Pacific daylight time
 —MST, EDT (*not* EDST)
stand by (*v.*), standby (*n.*), standbys
stand in (*v.*), stand-in (*n.*)
stand off (*v.*), standoff (*n.*)
Standoff, Alta.
stand out (*v.*), standout (*n.*)
standup (*n.* and *adj.*)
Stanley Cup
Star (*not* Star!) specialty channel
Stars and Stripes
startup (*n* and *adj.*)

state, New York state (geog.)
—State of New York (corp.)
—*but* in the state of New York
—state of the union message

Station—Capitalize as important building *but not*
when known by name of railway or town.
—Union Station
—the Via Rail station
—Mimico station

stationary (not moving)

stationery (writing materials)

Statistics Canada (*not* StatsCan *except in headlines*)

St. Bernard (dog)

St. Catharines, Ont.

St. Catharines Standard

STD (*use* sexually transmitted disease)

Ste-Catherine Street (Montreal)

steelworker

Stefansson, Vilhjalmur (explorer, 1879-1962)

Steinem, Gloria (feminist)

Stelco Inc. — now U.S. Steel Canada

stepdaughter, stepson, stepmother, stepfather *but*
step-parent

Stephenson, Sir William (1896-1989)

stepping-stone (*hyphen*)

Stetson (trademark)

St-Hyacinthe

still life, still lifes

stimulus, stimuli

St. James's Palace (London)

St-Jean, Que.

St-Jean-Baptiste Day (June 24, also Fête nationale)

St. John Ambulance

St. John of Jerusalem, Most Venerable Order of the
Hospital of (usually Order of St. John)

St. John River (N.B.)

St. John's, N.L.
St-Laurent, Louis
St. Lawrence Seaway, the seaway
  —St. Lawrence Seaway Authority
  —St. Lawrence Seaway Development Corp.
  (U.S.)
St. Marguerite Bourgeoys (Canada's first woman
  saint, 1620-1700)
St. Martin-in-the-Fields Church (London)
  —Academy of St. Martin-in-the-Fields
St. Marys, Ont.
stock exchange, Toronto Stock Exchange
stock market
stockpile (*one word*)
STOL (short takeoff and landing; *avoid*)
Stone Age
Stoney band (Alberta Indians), Stoneys
Stoney Creek, Ont. and N.B.
stony (*not* stoney)
Stony Lake (near Peterborough, Ont.)
Stony Mountain, Man.
Stony Plain, Alta.
Stony Point First Nation (southern Ontario)
storey (building), storeys
storm, hailstorm, rainstorm, snowstorm
storyteller, storytelling
St. Petersburg (formerly Leningrad)
St-Pierre-Miquelon (islands)
  —St-Pierre (capital city)
strafe, strafing
Strahl, Chuck (politician)
straightforward (*no hyphen*)
Strait—Capitalize when used with names.
  —Strait of Juan de Fuca
  —Georgia Strait
straitjacket

S

straitlaced

stratagem, stratagems

Stratas, Teresa (soprano)

strategic arms limitation talks (SALT)
>—SALT I, SALT II

Stratford Beacon Herald

Stratford Shakespeare Festival (*formerly* Stratford
>Festival)

Stratford upon Avon (Britain)
>—STRATFORD UPON AVON (in placelines)

stratum, strata

streamline (*one word*)

Street—Capitalize when used with names;
>abbreviate in numbered street addresses.
>—Bay Street, Wall Street
>—along Queen Street East
>—10 Queen St. E.
>—*but* 10 Downing Street (official residence)

streetcar (*one word*)

Streisand, Barbra

streptococcus, streptococci
>—*but* strep throat

strikebound (*no hyphen*)

strikebreaker (generally editorial; *use advisedly*)

striptease

strongman

strontium-90

Stroumboulopoulos, George

St. Thomas Times-Journal

St. Valentine's Day, Valentine's Day (Feb. 14)
>—*but* a valentine (card)

Styrofoam (trademark for a plastic foam)

suave, suavely, suaveness, suavity, suavities

subcommittee (*no hyphen*)

subcompact

sub judice (*two words, but avoid*)

sub-lieutenant (Sub-Lt.)

submachine-gun

subpoena (*n.* and *v.*), subpoenas, subpoenaed,
      subpoenaing

subtle, subtlety, subtleties

subtrade

succinct, succinctly

sudden infant death syndrome (SIDS OK *in second
      reference)*

suffragan (bishop)

Sukkot (Jewish festival)

sulfa drugs

sulphide, sulphite, sulphur

Sum 41 (performing group)

summer (season)

summerfallow

Summerside Journal-Pioneer

summit, summit conference (heads of government)

summons, summonses

summonsed (to appear in court)

sun

Suncor Energy Inc. (TSX:SU)
      —Sunoco (retail brand in Canada)

Sunni Muslim

Super Bowl

supercilious (*not* -silious)

superintendent, Supt. Herman Frank

supermarket (*one word)*

supersede

suppress, suppression, suppressor

supremacist (*not* supremist)

Supreme Court (federal, provincial, state)

Sûreté du Québec (*prefer* Quebec provincial police)

Suriname

SUV (sport utility vehicle)

Suzuki, David (geneticist)

swap (*not* swop)
SWAT (special weapons and tactics) team
sweatshirt
sweepstake
sweeten, sweetener, sweetening
sweetgrass
Sydney, N.S., and Australia, *but* Sidney, B.C.
Sydney Cape Breton Post
Sydney Steel Corp. (Sysco)
syllabus, syllabuses
symbol, symbolize
symmetrical, symmetry
symphony, Tchaikovsky's Fourth Symphony
symposium, symposiums
synagogue, Holy Blossom Synagogue
syndrome, Reye's, Down
synod, Anglican synod, General Synod
    —Lutheran Church — Missouri Synod
    (denom.)
    —Orthodox Holy Synod (Istanbul)
syphilis
Syrah (grape)
syrup (*not* sirup)
Sysco (Sydney Steel Corp.)

T, *as in* to a T
Tabasco (trademark for a hot sauce)
tableau, tableaus
taekwondo (*one word*)
tai chi (*two words*)
Taipei
Tajikistan, Tajik
take off (*v.*), takeoff (*n.*)
take out (*v.*), takeout (*n.*)
take over (*v.*), takeover (*n.*)
Taliban
Tamiflu (trademark for oseltamivir)
tangelo, tangelos
tank, M-60, PT-76, Leopard 1
targeted
tariff, Tariff Act
        —General Agreement on Tariffs and Trade
        (GATT)
tarsands (*one word*)
Taser (trademark — *Use* stun gun for generic
        reference)
task force (military term; *avoid overuse*)
tassel, tasselled
tastebuds
tattoo, tattooed
tax-free savings account (TFSA, *but avoid*)
T-ball
T-cell
Tchaikovsky, Peter (1840-1893)
TD Bank Financial Group (Toronto-Dominion Bank
        and its subsidiaries)
        —TD Canada Trust (banking)
        —TD Waterhouse (investing)
teammate (*no hyphen*)
Teamsters union (*acceptable in all references for*
        International Brotherhood of Teamsters,

Chauffeurs, Warehousemen and Helpers of America), a teamster (member of the union)

tear gas (*two words*)

technical sergeant (Tech. Sgt.)

Technicolor (trademark for a process of making colour movies)

Teck Cominco Ltd. (TSX:TCK.B)

teenage (*adj.*), teenager, teens

teenybopper

teepee

teetotal, teetotaller, teetotalism

Teflon (trademark for a non-stick coating)

Tehran

telecommunication

Telefilm Canada

Telephone numbers—Use hyphen, not brackets or spaces to break up: 1-519-228-6262, 1-800-268-9237.

TelePrompTer (trademark)

Telex (trade name)

telltale (*no hyphen*)

Telus Corp. (TSX:T)

Temagami, Ont. (*not* Tim-)

Témiscaming, Que. (town)

Témiscamingue (Que. county, electoral district)

Ten Commandments
     —Second Commandment

tendency (*not* -ancy), tendencies

tendon, Achilles tendon, *but* tendinitis

ten-gallon hat

Tennant, Veronica (ballet)

Tennessee (Tenn.)

tenpins (bowling)

tenterhooks (*not* tender-)

Teresa, Mother (1910-1997)

terminus, terminuses

T

Terry Fox Run
testament, Old Testament
Test match (cricket, rugby)
    —England-Australia Test match
    —the Test
Tetra Pak (cardboard-based packaging)
Texas (*no abbvn.*)
textbook
text message, messaging
thalidomide
Thanksgiving Day (Canada, second Monday in
    October; U.S., last Thursday in November)
the (*lowercase*) Netherlands
    —UTRECHT, Netherlands (placeline)
The—Capitalize at the beginning of the titles of
    books, magazines, movies, TV programs,
    songs, paintings and other compositions.
    Don't capitalize at the start of the names
    of almanacs, the Bible, directories,
    encyclopedias, gazetteers and handbooks.
The Associated Press (AP)
    —The Associated Press says ...
    —*but* the Associated Press reporter
Theatre—Capitalize as important buildings.
    —National Arts Centre
    —Princess of Wales Theatre
theatregoer
The Canadian Press (CP)
    —The Canadian Press says ...
    —*but* the Canadian Press reporter
The Hague
The Pas, Man.
therapeutic
thesis, theses
the West Indies
think-tank

T

Third World
Thompson, Greg (politician)
Thomson, R.H. (actor)
Thomson, Tom (painter, 1877-1917)
Thomson Reuters Corp. (TSX:TRI)
     —Thomson, Ken (1923-2006)
thoroughbred, standardbred
Thousand Islands (Ontario)
3-D
Three Wise Men
threshold
throne speech, speech from the throne
Thunder Bay Chronicle-Journal
Tiananmen Square
Ticketmaster *but* TicketsNow
tick-tack-toe (game)
tidbit
tie, tying
tiebreaker (game)
tie up (*v.*), tie-up (*n.*)
Tilcho First Nation (Northwest Territories)
till, until, *not* 'til
time, daylight, standard
     —eastern daylight time (EDT)
     —Pacific standard time (PST)
     —7 a.m., 6 p.m., 12:30 p.m.
timeline *(one word)*
Time magazine
Times (of London), the
time-slot
Time Warner Inc.
Tim Hortons (*no apostrophe,* TSX:THI)
     —a Tim Hortons shop
Timiskaming (Ontario lake and district)
Timiskaming-Cochrane (federal riding in Ontario)
Timiskaming reserve (Quebec)

Timorese (*n.* and *adj.*)

Titles—Capitalize formal titles when preceding names, not when following or when set off by commas: Judge John Jones; a judge, John Jones, spoke. But lowercase titles used with former, one-time, -elect, designate and similar adjectives, as former president Bill Clinton, former prime minister Jean Chretien, prime minister-designate Julie Smith. Lowercase mere occupation (GM president John Wong, bus driver Ron Brown) and in sport stories (captain Kathleen Keenan).

TiVo (trademark for brand of digital video recorder)

Tkachuk, David (senator)

TNT (trinitrotoluene)

T.O. (nickname for Toronto)

to a T

toboggan

Toews, Vic (politician)

Toews, Miriam (writer)

tomato, tomatoes

ton (2,000 pounds), long ton (2,240 pounds), tonne (1,000 kilograms or 2,204.62 pounds)
— *Use* ton, not tonne, in colloquial references (he weighed a ton; fell like a ton of bricks).

toonie, toonies ($2 coin)

top-notch (*adj.*)

tornado, tornadoes

Toronto St. Michael's Majors (hockey team)

Toronto Stock Exchange
—S&P/TSX composite index
—TMX Group Inc. (corporation, TSX:X)
—TSX Venture Exchange

Torstar Corp. (TSX:TS.B)

total, totalled

Touch-Tone (trademark for push-button dialling)

T

tourniquet

tower, CN Tower, Eiffel Tower

town, Town of Elmira (corp.)
> —*but* in the town of Elmira

township, Wilmot Township
> —*but* in the township of Wilmot

Toys "R" Us

trademark, trade name

traffic, trafficker, trafficking

traitor, traitorous

tranquillity

tranquillizer

TransAlta Corp. (TSX:TA)

transatlantic, transpacific

TransCanada Corp. (TSX:TRP)
> —TransCanada PipeLines Ltd. (TSX:TCA.
> PR.X)

Trans-Canada Highway

transcontinental (*no hyphen*)

Transcontinental Inc. (TSX:TCL.A)

trans fat (*two words*)

transfer, transferred

transgender (*adj., preferred to* transgendered)

Transkei (former homeland state in South Africa)

translator (*not* -er)

transpacific

Transportation Safety Board

Transport Canada

trauma, traumas, traumatic

travel, traveller, traveller's cheques

Treasury Board, Treasury Board President Vic
> Toews

treaty, Columbia River Treaty
> —Treaty 6 (*not* Six)

Treehouse TV

tremor

trendsetter, trendsetting
Tribune, La (newspaper in Sherbrooke, Que.)
triple-A (bonds, sports leagues)
Triple Crown (horse racing)
triple-decker
Triple-E Senate
TriStar (Lockheed aircraft)
Trivial Pursuit (trademark board game)
Trois-Rivières, Que.
trooper (military, *no abbvn.*), trouper (a staunch
    colleague — a "real trouper")
Trophy—Capitalize specific names.
    —Vézina Trophy
    —a championship trophy
Trudeau, Pierre Elliott (1919-2000)
Trudeau, Alexandre (*preferred to* Sacha)
Truman, Harry S. (1884-1972)
trustee, trustee Joanne Rocci
Tsawwassen, B.C.
T-shirt
tsunami (wave), tsunamis *(pl.)*
Tsuu T'ina Nation (aboriginal band)
TSX (Toronto Stock Exchange)
    —TSX Venture Exchange (junior exchange)
    —S&P/TSX composite index
Tube (London subway; also Underground)
tug of war (*no hyphens*)
Tuktoyaktuk, N.W.T.
tumour *but* tumorous
tune-up (*n.*)
tupek (Inuit equivalent of teepee, wigwam)
tuque (knitted cap; otherwise toque)
Turin, Italy
turkey, turkeys
Turkmenistan
Turp, Daniel (politician)

T

turtleneck sweater (*no hyphen*)
Tussaud's, Madame (wax museum in London)
      —*but* Louis Tussaud's Waxworks (Niagara
      Falls, Ont.)
Tutankhamen
Tutor (training jet)
TVA Group Inc. (TSX:TVA.B)
TV dinner
TV Land (specialty channel)
TVOntario, TVO
tween, tweens (usually eight- to 14-year-olds)
Twelfth Night
Twelve Apostles, the
two, twos
20th Century Fox (*no hyphen*)
tying (*not* tieing)
typeface
Type 1, Type 2 diabetes
typhoon Alice

U

U-boat
UFO(s) (unidentified flying object(s))
U.K. (*use periods*)
Ukraine (*not* the Ukraine)
Ukrainian
ultimatum, ultimatums
ultra-Orthodox (Jews)
ultrasound
Ultrasuede (trademark for a mock suede)
ultra vires (beyond the powers, *but avoid*)
umiak (Inuit open boat)
Umlaut—Indicate in German names by placing letter
"e" after vowel affected.
—Goebbels for Göbbels
—Duesseldorf for Düsseldorf
unabomber (Theodore Kaczynski)
unchristian, *but* non-Christian
unco-operative
unco-ordinated
underprivileged
undersecretary (*one word*)
underway
unforeseen
unforgivable (*not* -eable)
UNICEF (*OK in first reference*)
uninterested (not interested), disinterested (impartial)
union, state of the union message
Union Jack
Union Nationale
Union of Soviet Socialist Republics, former (U.S.S.R.,
Soviet Union)
United Appeal campaign
United Church of Canada
United Kingdom—England, Scotland, Wales and
Northern Ireland. But use "British government"
and such in preference to "United Kingdom

government."
-U.K. *(periods)*
United Nations (UN)
 —Food and Agriculture Organization of the United Nations (FAO, *but avoid*)
 —General Assembly
 —International Bank for Reconstruction and Development (World Bank)
 —International Civil Aviation Organization (ICAO)
 —International Court of Justice (*no abbvn.*)
 —International Labour Organization (ILO)
 —International Monetary Fund (IMF)
 —Office for the Co-ordination of Humanitarian Affairs (OCHA, *but avoid*)
 —Security Council
 —UN Children's Fund (UNICEF)
 —UN Educational, Scientific and Cultural Organization (UNESCO)
 —UN High Commissioner for Refugees
 —World Food Program
 —World Health Organization (WHO)
University—Capitalize the names of universities and colleges.

 —Memorial University
 —Simon Fraser University
 —Regis College
Lowercase departments, programs and courses.
 —political science department
 —native studies course
 —faculty of education
Unknown Soldier
unmistakable (*not* -eable)
unshakable (*not* -eable)
unwieldy

Upper Canada (region; name for Ontario
    1791-1841)
uppercase (*n.* and *v.*)
upper house, chamber
Upstate New York
Uranium One Inc. (TSX: UUU)
URL (uniform or universal resource locator)
US (use only with dollar figures: US$550)
usable (*not* useable)
usage (*not* useage)
US Airways
USA Today
U.S. Steel Canada (formerly Stelco Inc.)
usurer, usurious, usury
Utah (no abbvn.)
U-turn
Uzbekistan, Uzbek (*n.* and *adj.*)

V

vacillate

vacuum

Val-d'Isère

valentine (card)
> —*but* Valentine's Day

Valhalla

Valium (trademark for a tranquillizer)

Valkyrie

valley, Fraser Valley

valour *but* valorous

Van, Von—When lowercase in names, capitalize only at start of sentences. Van in Vietnamese names is uppercase.

Vancouver Grizzlies (former basketball team)

Van Doo (nickname of Quebec's Royal 22e Regiment)
> —Van Doos (personnel of the regiment)
> —Van Doo (one member)

van Gogh, Vincent (1853-1890)

Vanier, Georges (1888-1967)

VANOC (organizing committee for the Vancouver 2010 Olympics)

vapour, vapourish *but* vaporous, vaporize

Vaseline (trademark for a petroleum jelly)

Vatican II, Second Vatican Council

vaudeville

V-chip (television)

VCR (videocassette recorder)

Veda (scripture of Hinduism)

VE-Day, VJ-Day (for Victory in Europe Day, Victory in Japan Day)

Velcro (trademark)

venetian blind

ventilator (*not* respirator)

veranda (*not* -ah)

verbatim (*not* -um)

V

Vermilion, Alta.

Vermont (Vt.)

Versus—Use the abbreviation vs. only in sports
  schedules, agate and the names of court cases.

vertebra, vertebrae

Veterans Affairs Canada (*no apostrophe)*

veterinarian

Vézina Trophy

Viagra (impotence drug)

Via Rail (*not* VIA)

vice (bad habit), vise (clamp)

vice-admiral (*no abbvn.*)

vice-president
  —U.S. Vice-President James Smith
  —former U.S. vice-president Al Gore
  —GM vice-president Joan Arthur

vice versa (*two words*)

vichyssoise

vicious

Vickers, Jon (tenor)

Victoria Cross (VC)

Victoria Times Colonist

vidalia onion

video, videocassette, videocassette recorder (VCR),
  videotape, video game

Videotron (cable provider owned by Quebecor Inc.)

vie, *but* vying

Vietnam, Vietnamese

vigour, vigorous

vilify

village, Village of Bridgeport (corp.)
  —*but* in the village of Bridgeport

VIP (for very important person), VIPs

Virgin (Christ's mother)

Virginia (Va.)

Virgin Islands (*no abbvn.*)

V

virtuoso, virtuosos
Visa (credit card)
vis-a-vis
viscount, Viscount Montgomery
viscous (sticky)
vise (clamp), vice (bad habit)
Vishnu
VisionTV (specialty channel)
vitamin B
Vizinczey, Stephen (novelist)
VJ (*not* veejay), VJs, VJing
VLT (video lottery terminal)
V-neck
vociferous
voice mail (*two words*)
Voice of Women (VoW)
voice-over-Internet protocol (VoIP *in second
    reference*)
Voisey's Bay (Labrador)
Voix de l'Est, La (newspaper in Granby, Que.)
volatile
volcano, volcanoes
Volkswagen
vomit, vomited, vomiting
Von, Van—When lowercase in names, capitalize
    only at start of sentence except for van in
    Vietnamese names, which is uppercase.
    —Kai-Uwe von Hassel (Germany)
    —Nguyen Van Hai (Vietnam)
vow (solemn oath; often misused)
vs. (abbreviation for versus, used only in sports
    schedules, agate and the names of court cases)

wacky (*not* whacky)

wagon, bandwagon, chuckwagon, station wagon

wake-up call

Walesa, Lech

walkie-talkie

Walkman (trademark for headset stereo)

walk out (*v.*), walkout (*n.*)

Walkuere, Die (Wagner opera)

wall, Berlin Wall, Great Wall of China, Wailing Wall
(in Jerusalem; *prefer* Western Wall), Wall Street

Wal-Mart

 —Wal-Mart Canada, Wal-Mart (in Canada)

 —Wal-Mart Stores Inc. (U.S. corporate entity)

 —Walmart (brand name in U.S.)

War—Capitalize major armed conflicts.

 —Civil War (U.S.)

 —First World War (*not* World War I)

 —Persian Gulf War

 —Second World War (*not* World War II)

 —*but* a third world war

 —Six-Day War

 —Korean War

 —Vietnam War

 —Wars of the Roses

 —cod war

 —tariff war

 —Cold War (fanciful term)

Ward 2

warhorse, warlord, warmonger

Warner Bros. Entertainment (division of AOL Time
Warner)

warrant officer (*no abbvn.*)

 —chief warrant officer

 —master warrant officer

Warsaw Pact, former

wartime

Washington, D.C.
Washington (Wash.)
WASP (white Anglo-Saxon Protestant)
Wassermann test
wastebasket
Wasylycia-Leis, Judy (politician)
watchdog
waterfowl
Waterloo, University of (*not* Waterloo University)
Waterloo Region Record; the Record, of Waterloo
    Region
water-ski, water-skiing
wavelength
web, web browser, webcam, webcast, web-enabled,
    webmaster, web page, web server, website but
    World Wide Web
Web Addresses—It is not necessary to include
    http://. But do include less familiar common
    forms such as ftp://. Follow upper and
    lowercase: www.thecanadianpress.com.
    When a company uses its web address as
    its corporate name, capitalize the first letter:
    Amazon.com.
Week—Capitalize special events: Earth Week.
weekday, weekend, weeklong (*one word*)
weird, weirdo
Welch (regiment names)
    —*but* Welsh Guards
Welland Canal
well-being (*hyphen*)
welsh (on a bet; *avoid*)
Welsh (folk, tongue)
Welshpool, N.B. (*not* Welch-)
West—Capitalize regions but not their derivatives.
    Lowercase mere direction or position.
    —the West (region of Canada or the world)

—the richest countries in the West
—the richest western countries
—The West won the Grey Cup.
—a westerner
—one western MP
—Western Canada
—a western Canadian
—the western Canadian provinces
—the western provinces
—western premiers
—in western Manitoba
—The snow moved west across Western Canada.
—West Coast (region)
—west coast (shoreline)
—the East-West talks
—western Europe
—western leaders
—western France
—Western Hemisphere

West, Wild

West Bank (of the River Jordan)

West End (London theatre district)

western (movie, book)

WestJet Airlines Ltd. (TSX:WJA)

Westminster, Westminster Abbey (London), New Westminster, B.C.

Westmorland County (N.B. and England)

West Nile virus

Weston, Hilary

West Virginia (W.Va.)

Weyerhaeuser Co. Ltd.

W-Five

wharf, wharfs

Wheat—Capitalize varieties generally except where usage has established the lowercase; Selkirk, *but* durum.

wheelchair

whereabouts (usually takes a singular verb)

Whibley, Deryck (Sum 41)

whip, party whip John O'Neill

whiskey (Irish and American); whisky (Scottish and
Canadian); whiskies

whistleblower *(no hyphen)*

Whitehorse, Yukon

White House

white paper (a report issued by government to
provide information)

whiz, whiz-kid

whodunit *(not -nn-)*

Whycocomagh (First Nations band on Cape Breton)

wide *(suffix)*, citywide, worldwide, provincewide,
countrywide *(avoid* nationwide when
countrywide is meant), Canada-wide

widescreen

wield

wiener, wiener schnitzel

Wi-Fi (wireless fidelity; prefer description such as
wireless network *in first reference*)

wigwag *(no hyphen)*

Wi-LAN Inc. (TSX:WIN)

Wild West

Wilfrid Laurier University

wilful *(not* willful)

Wimbledon tennis championships

wing commander (Wing Cmdr.)

winter (season)

Winter Olympic Games, the Winter Games, the
Games

Wisconsin (Wis.)

wit, halfwit, halfwitted
—at his wit's end

withdraw, withdrawal
withhold
W Network (TV)
Wojtyla, Karol (Pope John Paul II, 1978-2005)
Woman—Don't use as an adjective unless
    man would be used in similar fashion
    (womenswear, menswear). *Prefer* female if it
    is necessary to specify sex.
    —female astronaut, *not* woman astronaut
Woman's Christian Temperance Union (*not*
    Women's)
womenswear, menswear
woollen, woolly
Workers' Compensation, Health and Safety Board
    (Yukon)
Workers' Compensation Board (*with apostrophe*
    in Alberta, British Columbia, Northwest
    Territories and Nunavut, Nova Scotia,
    Saskatchewan)
Workers Compensation Board (*no apostrophe* in
    Manitoba, Prince Edward Island)
workforce
workload
workplace
Workplace Health, Safety and Compensation
    Commission (New Brunswick,
    Newfoundland and Labrador)
Workplace Safety and Insurance Board (Ontario)
world
    —Old World, New World
    —free world (*but avoid*)
    —Third World
World Bank
World Cup (soccer)
World Health Organization (WHO)
World Series (baseball), the Series

world's fair, Montreal, New York
      —Expo 67, Expo 86 (*no apostrophe*)
World Trade Center (New York)
worldwide (*one word*)
World Wide Web, the web
World Wildlife Fund (*not* federation)
worshippers
worthwhile
write down (*v.*), writedown (*n.*)
write off (*v.*), writeoff (*n.*)
wrongdoer, wrongdoing, wrongful
Wrzesnewskyj, Borys (MP)
Wyoming (Wyo.)

X-Acto (trademark for knives)
Xbox
X chromosome, Y chromosome
Xerox (trademark for a photocopier, etc.)
X-Files, The
Xinhua News Agency (official agency of Chinese
    government)
X-rated (movie)
X-ray (*n.* and *v.*)
Xstrata Nickel (formerly Falconbridge; now
    division of Xstrata PLC)
yahoo
Yahoo Inc. (*not* Yahoo! Inc.)
Yahweh
Yamani, Sheik Ahmed Zaki
Yangon (formerly Rangoon)
Yankee
yarmulke (skullcap)
Year, Man of the, Newsmaker of the
Yellowhead Pass
yenta
Y-Flyer (sailboat)
YMCA (Young Men's Christian Association)
yogurt
Yom Kippur
Youth Criminal Justice Act (replaced Young
    Offenders Act (*no apostrophe)* in April 2003)
YouTube
yo-yo, yo-yos
Yukon, the (*no abbvn.*)
    —*but* Yukon in placelines: FARO, Yukon
yule, yuletide
yuppie (young urban professional)
YWCA (Young Women's Christian Association)
Zaire (now Congo)
Zamboni (trademark for ice-surfacing machine)

X-Y-Z

Zellers (*no apostrophe*)
Zen Buddhism
zero, zeros
Zhou Enlai (1898-1976, formerly Chou En-lai)
zidovudine (HIV-AIDS drug, also called AZT)
zigzag (*no hyphen*)
Zimbabwe
Zinfandel
Zion, Zionism, Zionist
zip code (U.S.)
Znaimer, Moses (television)
zodiac
zoologist, zoology
zucchini

Numbers

Act 1, the first act
Article 8, Art. 8
behind the 8-ball
C (used only with dollar figures: C$1,386)
Category 3
CBC Radio One, Radio Two
Cell Block 5
cents, nine cents, 43 cents
Channel 2 (television)
Chapter 2
Chemical elements—Write out *in first reference* (carbon dioxide) but symbols *OK in second reference* if popularly used: CO_2.
Chromosome 7
Cloud 9
Day 1
Detroit Three automakers
55 BC; AD 1978
four-by-four (four-wheel-drive vehicle)
4-for-5 (four hits in five at-bats)
4-H
49th parallel
Fractions—Use figures for all numbers with fractions (9 3/4). Spell out and hyphenate common fractions used alone (three-quarters).
Grade 7
G7, G8 (group of countries)
karat, 14-karat gold
Latitude, Longitude—44 degrees north, 49 degrees 30 minutes west, etc.
Leopard 1 (tank)
line 46
911 (emergency calls), 9-11 (for day of terrorist attacks in United States)
1930s, '30s
—*but* Expo 67, Expo 86 (*no apostrophe*)

Numbers

1920-21, *but* 1999-2003

No. 1, number 1 (*not* number one)

10 Downing Street (*exception*)

10th (*no period*)

page 23, p. 23

paragraph 3

Phase 1 (drug trials, etc.)

Room 14

Scene 3, the third scene

season 2

Section 8, Sec. 8

7Up (soft drink)

Telephone numbers—Use hyphens, not spaces
   or brackets to break up: 416-228-6262,
   1-888-268-9237.

3-D

Treaty 6

24-7 (24 hours a day, seven days a week, *but avoid*)

24 Sussex Drive (*exception*)

2,4-D (weed killer)

two-by-four

20-something, 30-something

20th century

20th Century Fox

US (used only with dollar figures: US$295)

verse 3

VIII (*no period*)

V-6, V-8 (engine)

Plain Words

When there is a choice of words, prefer the short to the long, the familiar to the unfamiliar. This chapter lists some long or formal words along with some shorter or more familiar alternatives that may do the job better.

abandon	leave, quit, give up
abbreviate	shorten, cut
abduct	kidnap, seize
abolish	end, do away with, scrap
abrasion	scrape, scratch
accelerate	hurry, speed up
accessible	easily reached, ready, at hand
accommodate	house, shelter, put up
accordingly	so, therefore
according to	under; say
accumulate	pile up, collect
acknowledge	admit, concede
acquire	buy, gain, get
acquit	free, clear, release
additional	added, more, extra
in addition to	besides
adhere	stick, cling
adjacent	beside, next to, touching
administer	manage, direct, control
adverse	harmful, damaging
advise	tell, write, inform
advocate	support, call for
affluent	rich, well-to-do
aggravate	annoy, provoke, worsen
aggressive	pushing, pushy
alienate	put off, turn against
allegiance	loyalty
alleviate	ease, soften
alteration	change, revision

Plain Words

alternate	take turns
alternative	choice, other
amalgamate	unite, combine
amendment	change, revision
amicable	friendly, pleasant
anonymous	nameless, unknown
antagonize	offend, anger
apparent	clear, plain, obvious
appreciative	grateful, thankful
appropriate	fit, proper
approximately	about
aptitude	gift, knack, talent
arguably	perhaps, maybe
as far as... is concerned	as to
asphyxiate	choke, suffocate
assist	help, aid
astute	shrewd, clever
attempt	try
attired	dressed, wearing
authentic	genuine, real, true
authorize	approve, allow, give power
autonomous	free, independent, self-governing
available	ready, on hand
bargain	deal
beneficial	good for, helpful, useful
bereavement	death, loss
beverage	drink
biannual	twice a year, every two years
bigotry	bias, narrow-mindedness, racism
bilateral	two-sided
bona fide	real, in good faith
capacity	ability, position, space, size

Plain Words

catastrophe	disaster
cease	stop, end
censure	blame, scold
characteristic	trait, mark, feature
circumstance	event, condition, fact
clad	dressed, wearing
coagulate	clot, congeal
coerce	force, press
collaborate	work together, team up
comatose	unconscious
commence	begin, start
commitment	promise, pledge
communicable	catching, infectious
communicate	tell, inform, write, telephone
comparable	like, similar
compensate	pay, make up
competent	able, trained
complete	fill out, finish
complimentary	free
comply	follow, obey, give in
compulsion	urge
conceive	think up, imagine, dream up
concerning	about, for, on
conclude	end
concur	agree, match
conduct	carry on, do, run
confederation	alliance, league, union
congenital	inborn, inbred
conscientious	careful, painstaking
consequently	so
considerable	much, ample
consolation	comfort, relief, help
conspicuous	plain, obvious
constitute	are, make up, form

Plain Words

construct	build, make
consult	ask, talk over
consume	eat, use up
contaminate	taint, pollute, dirty, poison
contemplate	consider, study, weigh
contribute	give, share, help
controversy	debate, issue
contusion	bruise
convenient	useful, handy
convulsion	seizure, spasm
corroborate	confirm, verify
counterfeit	false, phoney, fake
courteous	polite
criterion	test, rule, model, yardstick
currently	now
deactivate	shut off, close
dearth	lack, shortage, scarcity
deceased	dead
decompose	rot, decay
decontaminate	purify, disinfect, sterilize
decrease	cut, drop, fall
decry	blame, condemn
de-emphasize	play down, softpedal
de facto	actual, real
defective	faulty, broken
deficient	lacking, poor
defraud	cheat, swindle, fleece
demonstrate	show, prove
depart	go, leave, check out
deplete	empty, sap, reduce
depreciate	lessen, cheapen, scorn
depressed	backward, diminished, sad
designate	name, call, label
destitute	poor, needy, bare
determine	fix, test, find out, decide, settle

development	growth, change
deviate	swerve, stray, turn aside, vary
dimension	size
diminutive	tiny
disallow	turn down, reject
discontinue	end, give up, stop
disembark	get off, leave, land
disguise	hide, mask
disintegrate	fall apart, crumble, break up
dispatch	send, issue
display	show, bare
distinguish	tell apart, make out
distribute	hand out, spread
divulge	tell, give, reveal
don	put on, get into
donation	gift, present
draconian	harsh
dubious	unsure, doubtful
duplicate	copy, repeat
dwell	live, occupy
eccentric	odd, strange
economical	thrifty, cheap
edifice	building
elevate	lift, raise
eliminate	get rid of, throw out, drop
emaciated	gaunt, bony, thin, wasted
eminent	famous, high, noted
emphasize	stress, underline
empirical	practical
employ	use, hire, apply
encounter	meet, come upon
endorsement	support, backing
enhance	add to, improve
ensue	follow, develop

Plain Words

enumerate	count, add up, cite
envisage	see, foresee, imagine
escalate	step up, intensify
eschew	avoid
in the event of	if
evident	plain, obvious
excessive	too much, undue
in excess of	over
exhibit	show, reveal, display
exonerate	free, clear, acquit
exorbitant	excessive, too high, overpriced
expedite	speed up, push
expenditure	spending, expense, cost
experience	feel, live through, undergo
expertise	skill, knowledge, know-how
explicit	clear, precise, exact
extended	long, drawn out
extensive	large, wide, broad, roomy
exterminate	wipe out, destroy
extinguish	put out, douse, smother
fabricate	make, build; lie, trump up
facilitate	ease, make easy, help, lighten
failed to	did not
fallacy	error, fault, pitfall
feasible	possible, can be done, workable
finalize	finish, complete, end
fluctuate	rise and fall, swing, waver
fortunate	lucky, happy
fracture	break
frequently	often
frustration	defeat, dismay
fundamental	basic, real

Plain Words

generate	produce, cause
gratuity	gift, tip
on the grounds that	because
hazardous	unsafe, risky, dangerous
ideology	beliefs
illumination	light, insight
illustration	example, picture, drawing
immediately	at once, now
immense	huge, vast
immovable	set, firm, fixed
impartial	neutral, fair, just
impeccable	flawless, perfect
impede	slow, hamper, stall, hinder
imperative	urgent, vital, pressing
imperceptible	slight, subtle, hidden
impersonate	copy, mimic
impetus	spur, push, urge
implement	do, set up, begin, carry out
impolite	rude
impostor	cheat, fraud, ringer
impotent	weak, helpless, powerless
inaccuracy	mistake, error
inadvertent	accidental, careless
inadvisable	unwise, risky
inaugurate	begin, launch
in camera	private
incapacitate	disable, damage, lay up
incarcerate	jail, intern, imprison
incision	cut, slit
incite	rouse, prod, goad
inclement	stormy, harsh, nasty
incompetent	unfit, inept
inconceivable	incredible, beyond belief
incorrect	wrong
increase	rise, go up, gain, grow
incredulous	dubious, skeptical

Plain Words

indefinite	vague, uncertain, dim
independent	free; well-off
indicate	show, suggest, hint, imply
indigenous	native
indignant	angry, upset
indispensable	vital, crucial, essential
individual	person, man, woman
ineligible	unfit, unsuitable
inevitable	sure, destined
inexpensive	cheap, low-priced, modest
inflexible	rigid, firm, stiff
inform	tell
ingenious	clever, deft, masterly
inherent	inborn, inbred, essential
inhibit	check, hinder, curb
initial	first
initiate	begin, open
injunction	ban, order
in lieu of	instead of
innate	inborn, natural
innovation	change, novelty
input	say, opinion, suggestion
inquire	ask
insecure	unsafe, unsure
institute	set up, begin, found
instrument	tool, agent, means
insufficient	not enough, short
insurrection	revolt, riot, mutiny
integrate	absorb, combine, mix
intention	aim, plan, goal, purpose
interface	work together, connect
intermission	pause, break
interrogate	question, pump, quiz
interrupt	break in, butt in, hinder, stop
intersection	corner

Plain Words

inundate	flood, deluge, overflow, engulf
irrelevant	beside the point, off-base
irresponsible	careless, rash, reckless
jurisdiction	control, power, domain
laceration	cut, tear, gash
latitude	scope, range
laud	praise
lenient	mild, gentle, sparing
liberate	free, rescue
locality	place, spot, site
locate	find, pinpoint
lubricate	oil, grease
magnitude	size, extent
majority	most, bulk, mass
manufacture	make, produce, build
maximum	most, biggest, longest
meaningful	big, important, significant
medication	medicine, remedy, pill, drug
mediocre	ordinary, run-of-the-mill
mentality	mind, frame of mind, outlook
methodology	method
milieu	setting, scene; culture
minimal	small, token
minimize	lessen, play down, belittle, diminish
minuscule	tiny
mitigate	ease, soften, make mild, temper
modification	change
momentous	important
motivate	inspire, drive, cause
narrate	tell, recount, relate
nauseous	sickening, repulsive

Plain Words

necessitate	need, compel, call for
negligent	careless
negotiate	bargain, talk business
neo-natal	newborn
neophyte	novice, beginner, learner, apprentice
neutralize	offset, cancel
nominal	small, token
notification	notice, warning
numerous	many
nurture	feed, train
nutritious	nourishing, wholesome
objective	end, aim, goal, mission
obligation	duty, debt
oblige	compel, force
obscure	dim, hidden
observation	remark, comment
obsolescent	dying out, disappearing
obsolete	worn-out, disused, out-of-date
obstruction	barrier, block, hurdle
obtain	get, come by, gain
occasion	event, cause, chance
occupation	job, trade, profession
occurrence	event, incident
ongoing	continuing, active, permanent
operate	work, run; cut out, remove
opportunity	chance
optimal	best
option	choice
originate	invent, create
outrageous	shocking, disgusting
overabundance	abundance, excess, glut
overview	view, survey
palatable	tasty, pleasing, sweet

Plain Words

panache	dash, pizzazz, zip
parameter	limit, boundary
paraphrase	reword, restate
parochial	narrow
participate	take part, share in, join in
pending	until, in the air
perceive	see, view, regard
periphery	edge, outskirts
permanent	lasting, endless
permission	consent, go-ahead
perquisite	perk, fringe benefit, right
persevere	persist, hold on, endure, stand
perspiration	sweat
persuade	win over, sway, coax
pertinent	fit, right, apt
philosophy	idea, view, system
physician	doctor
place	put
pollute	dirty, poison, taint
portion	part, piece, share
position	job
possess	own, have
postpone	put off, shelve, delay
practicable	workable, can be done
pragmatic	practical
preclude	prevent, shut out, avert
predicament	difficulty
prejudicial	harmful
preliminary to	before
preparedness	readiness
prerogative	privilege, right
presently	soon
prestigious	honoured, famous
principal	main, chief
prior to	before

Plain Words

probability	likelihood, chance
procedure	way, course, method
proceed	go
proficient	skilled, deft, masterly
prohibit	ban, prevent, forbid
project	plan
proliferation	spread
prophesy	foretell, predict
proponent	advocate, supporter
proposal	plan, offer
prosthesis	artificial limb
protocol	etiquette, usage
provide	give, offer, have, say
proviso	condition
provoke	stir up, annoy, tease
prowess	skill, talent
purchase	buy
for the purpose of	to
qualification	ability, skill, requirement
quandary	difficulty, impasse
radiant	bright, glowing
rampant	rife, raging, unchecked
ratification	assent, acceptance, approval
rationale	reason, thinking, theory
reciprocate	return, share
reconnaissance	survey, scrutiny
recuperate	recover, get well, rally
reduction	cut
redundant	extra, not needed
with regard to	on, about, as to
regimen	rule, system; diet
regret	be sorry
regulation	rule, law, bylaw
rehabilitate	redeem, straighten out, restore

Plain Words

reimburse	pay back, refund
reinforce	strengthen, brace, prop up
reiterate	repeat, say again
remainder	rest, others
remark	say
renegade	outlaw, crook, criminal
replica	copy, model
representative	agent, deputy
reprimand	rebuke, scold
repudiate	disown, reject, deny
require	need, call for, ask for
rescind	set aside, repeal, cancel
resemblance	likeness
reside	live, occupy, room
residence	house, home, apartment
respond	answer, reply
restrain	check, stop
retain	keep
retrench	cut down, reduce
retrieve	bring back, recover
reveal	show
rupture	break, snap
sanguine	optimistic, confident
sanitary	healthful, clean, germ-free
saturate	soak, fill, drench
segment	part
selection	choice, pick
self-confessed	confessed
significant	serious, grave
similar	like
situated	placed, put, housed
socialize	mingle, meet, make friends
solicit	ask for, beg, canvass
spacious	vast, roomy
state	say

Plain Words

stigma	stain, taint, disgrace
stimulate	arouse, stir up, excite
stringent	strict, tight
submit	give, send
subordinate	helper, assistant
subsequently	later, after that
substantiate	prove, support, back up
sufficient	enough, plenty, ample
suffocate	smother, choke
summon	send for
superficial	shallow, slight, flimsy
supersede	replace, displace
in short supply	scarce
supportive of	support
sustain	suffer, bear
syndrome	symptoms, clue
systematic	orderly, regular
technicality	detail, minor point
temperamental	moody, fickle, high-strung
terminal	fatal
terminate	end, stop
therapeutic	healing
toxic	poisonous, deadly
transform	change, alter
transmit	send
transparent	clear, lucid
traumatic	shocking
turbulent	stormy, wild, violent
ulterior	hidden
ultimate	last, final
underprivileged	poor, hard up
unfavourable	harmful, damaging
unmistakable	clear, plain, evident
unpretentious	modest, humble
unveil	announce
updated	current

upgrade	improve, better
urbane	polished, well-bred, elegant
utilize	use
vacillate	waver, falter, hesitate
validity	truth, proof
vaunted	celebrated, famous
vehicle	car, truck, bus
velocity	speed
venue	place, site
verbatim	word for word, exactly
viable	workable, practical, usable
vicinity	near, close
visualize	see, foresee, imagine, picture
vulnerable	defenceless
withhold	hold back, refuse
withstand	bear, endure, resist, cope

TSX-listed Companies

A list of the major publicly traded companies, with their stock code, on the Toronto Stock Exchange:

ACE Aviation Holdings Inc.	ACE.B
Addax Petroleum Corp.	AXC
Advantage Energy Income Fund	AVN.UN
Aecon Group Inc.	ARE
AGF Management Ltd.	AGF.B
Agnico-Eagle Mines	AEM
Agrium Inc.	AGU
Alamos Gold Inc.	AGI
Alimentation Couche-Tard Inc.	ATD.B
Altagas Income Trust	ALA.UN
ARC Energy Trust	AET.UN
Astral Media Inc.	ACM.A
Atco Ltd.	ACO.X
Bank Of Montreal	BMO
Bank Of Nova Scotia (The)	BNS
Barrick Gold Corp.	ABX
Baytex Energy Trust	BTE.UN
BCE Inc.	BCE
Bell Aliant Regional Communications Income Fund	BA.UN
BFI Canada Ltd.	BFC
Biovail Corp.	BVF
Birchcliff Energy Ltd.	BIR
Boardwalk REIT	BEI.UN
Bombardier Inc.	BBD.B
Bonavista Energy Trust	BNP.UN
Brookfield Asset Management Inc.	BAM.A
Brookfield Properties Corp.	BPO
CAE Inc.	CAE
Calfrac Well Services Ltd.	CFW
Calloway REIT	CWT.UN
Cameco Corp.	CCO
Canadian Apartment Properties REIT	CAR.UN

TSX-listed Companies

Canadian Hydro Developers, Inc.	KHD
Canadian Imperial Bank Of Commerce	CM
Canadian National Railway Company	CNR
Canadian Natural Resources Ltd.	CNQ
Canadian Oil Sands Trust	COS.UN
Canadian Pacific Railway Ltd.	CP
Canadian REIT	REF.UN
Canadian Tire Corp. Ltd.	CTC.A
Canadian Utilities Ltd.	CU
Canadian Western Bank	CWB
Canfor Corp.	CFP
Cardiome Pharma Corp.	COM
Cascades Inc.	CAS
CCL Industries Inc.	CCL.B
Celestica Inc.	CLS
CGI Group Inc.	GIB.A
Chartwell Seniors Housing REIT	CSH.UN
CI Financial Corp.	CIX
Cineplex Galaxy Income Fund	CGX.UN
CML Healthcare Income Fund Trust	CLC.UN
Cogeco Cable Inc.	CCA
Cominar REIT	CUF.UN
Connacher Oil & Gas Ltd.	CLL
Consumers' Waterheater Income Fund	CWI.UN
Corus Entertainment Inc.	CJR.B
Crescent Point Energy Trust	CPG.UN
Crew Energy Inc	CR
Davis & Henderson Income Fund	DHF.UN
Daylight Resources Trust	DAY.UN
Dorel Industries Inc.	DII.B
Dundee Corp.	DC.A
Eldorado Gold Corp.	ELD
Emera Inc.	EMA
Empire Company Ltd.	EMP.A
Enbridge Inc.	ENB
EnCana Corp.	ECA

TSX-listed Companies

Enerflex Systems Income Fund	EFX.UN
Energy Savings Income Fund	SIF.UN
Enerplus Resources Fund	ERF.UN
Ensign Energy Services Inc.	ESI
Epcor Power LP	EP.UN
Equinox Minerals Ltd.	EQN
European Goldfields Ltd.	EGU
Extendicare REIT	EXE.UN
Fairborne Energy Ltd.	FEL
Fairfax Financial Holdings Ltd.	FFH
Finning International Inc.	FTT
First Quantum Minerals Ltd.	FM
FirstService Corp.	FSV
FNX Mining Company Inc.	FNX
Fort Chicago Energy Partners LP	FCE.UN
Fortis Inc.	FTS
Forzani Group Ltd.	FGL
Freehold Royalty Trust	FRU.UN
Galleon Energy Inc.	GO
Gammon Gold Inc.	GAM
George Weston Ltd.	WN
Gerdau Ameristeel Corp.	GNA
Gildan Activewear Inc.	GIL
Goldcorp Inc.	G
Great-West Lifeco Inc.	GWO
Groupe Aeroplan Inc.	AER
H&R REIT	HR.UN
Harry Winston Diamond Corp.	HW
Harvest Energy Trust	HTE.UN
Highpine Oil & Gas Ltd.	HPX
Home Capital Group Inc.	HCG
HudBay Minerals Inc.	HBM
Husky Energy Inc.	HSE
Iamgold Corp.	IMG
IGM Financial Inc.	IGM
Imperial Oil Ltd.	IMO

TSX-listed Companies

Industrial Alliance Insurance and Financial Services Inc.	IAG
ING Canada Inc.	IIC
Inmet Mining Corp.	IMN
InnVest REIT	INN.UN
Inter Pipeline Fund LP	IPL.UN
InterOil Corp.	IOL
Iteration Energy Ltd.	ITX
Ivanhoe Mines Ltd.	IVN
Jazz Air Income Fund	JAZ.UN
Jean Coutu Group (PJC) Inc. (The)	PJC.A
Keyera Facilities Income Fund	KEY.UN
Kingsway Financial Services Inc.	KFS
Kinross Gold Corp.	K
Labrador Iron Ore Royalty Income Fund	LIF.UN
Laurentian Bank of Canada	LB
Loblaw Companies Ltd.	L
Lundin Mining Corp.	LUN
MacDonald Dettwiler and Associates	MDA
Magna International Inc.	MG.A
Major Drilling Group International Inc.	MDI
Manitoba Telecom Services Inc.	MBT
Manulife Financial Corp.	MFC
Maple Leaf Foods Inc.	MFI
MDS Inc.	MDS
Methanex Corp.	MX
Metro Inc.	MRU.A
Mullen Group Income Fund	MTL.UN
NAL Oil & Gas Trust	NAE.UN
National Bank Of Canada	NA
New Gold Inc.	NGD
Newalta Income Fund	NAL.UN
Nexen Inc.	NXY
Niko Resources Ltd.	NKO
Nortel Networks Corp.	NT
North West Company Fund	NWF.UN

TSX-listed Companies

Northbridge Financial Corp.	NB
Northland Power Income Fund	NPI.UN
Nova Chemicals Corp.	NCX
NuVista Enervy Ltd.	NVA
Oilexco Inc.	OIL
Onex Corp.	OCX
Open Text Corp.	OTC
Opti Canada Inc.	OPC
Pan American Silver Corp.	PAA
Paramount Energy Trust	PMT.UN
Paramount Resources Ltd.	POU
Pason Systems Inc.	PSI
Pembina Pipeline Income Fund	PIF.UN
Pengrowth Energy Trust	PGF.UN
Penn West Energy Trust	PWT.UN
Petrobank Energy & Resources Ltd.	PBG
Petro-Canada	PCA
Peyto Energy Trust	PEY.UN
Potash Corp. Of Saskatchewan Inc.	POT
Power Corp. Of Canada	POW
Power Financial Corp.	PWF
Precision Drilling Trust	PD.UN
Primaris Retail REIT	PMZ.UN
ProEx Energy Ltd.	PXE
Progress Energy Trust	PGX.UN
Provident Energy Trust	PVE.UN
Quadra Mining Ltd.	QUA
Quebecor Inc.	QBR.B
Red Back Mining Inc.	RBI
Reitman's (Canada) Ltd.	RET.A
Research In Motion Ltd.	RIM
Riocan REIT	REI.UN
Ritchie Bros. Auctioneers Inc.	RBA
Rogers Communications Inc.	RCI.B
Rona Inc.	RON
Royal Bank Of Canada	RY

TSX-listed Companies

Russel Metals Inc.	RUS
Saputo Inc.	SAP
Savanna Energy Services Corp.	SVY
Sears Canada Inc.	SCC
Shaw Communications Inc.	SJR.B
ShawCor Ltd.	SCL.A
Sherritt International Corp.	S
Shoppers Drug Mart Corp.	SC
Silver Standard Resources Inc.	SSO
Silver Wheaton Corp.	SLW
Silvercorp Metals Inc.	SVM
Sino-Forest Corp.	TRE
SNC-Lavalin Group Inc.	SNC
Stantec Inc.	STN
Sun Life Financial Inc.	SLF
Suncor Energy Inc.	SU
Superior Plus Income Fund	SPF.UN
Talisman Energy Inc.	TLM
Tanzanian Royalty Exploration Corp.	TNX
Teck Cominco Ltd.	TCK.B
Telus Corp.	T
Thompson Creek Metals Company Inc.	TCM
Thomson Reuters Corp.	TRI
Tim Hortons Inc.	THI
TimberWest Forest Corp.	TWF.UN
TMX Group Inc.	X
Toromont Industries Ltd.	TIH
Toronto-Dominion Bank	TD
Torstar Corp.	TS.B
TransAlta Corp.	TA
Transat A.T. Inc.	TRZ.B
TransCanada Corp.	TRP
Transcontinental Inc.	TCL.A
TransForce Inc.	TFI
Trican Well Service Ltd.	TCW
Trinidad Drilling Ltd.	TDG

TSX-listed Companies

TriStar Oil & Gas Ltd.	TOG
Uranium One Inc.	UUU
UTS Energy Corp.	UTS
Vermilion Energy Trust	VET.UN
Viterra Inc.	VT
West Fraser Timber Co Ltd.	WFT
WestJet Airlines Ltd.	WJA
Westshore Terminals Income Fund	WTE.UN
Yamana Gold Inc.	YRI
Yellow Pages Income Fund	YLO.UN

Notes

Notes

Notes

Other books from
The Canadian Press

The Canadian Press Stylebook

The Canadian Press Stylebook is the bible consulted by
journalists at Canada's national news agency as they
deliver hundreds of stories each day to newspapers,
broadcasters and Internet sites. The Stylebook
is a one-stop reference guide for writing cleanly,
accurately and concisely. It includes:

• Easy-to-follow guidelines on capitalization,
punctuation, abbreviations and other writing style
and editing issues.
• Chapters on the basics of being a journalist,
including reporting, handling breaking news,
interviewing techniques, political reporting,
headline writing and more.
• A chapter on writing for and about the Internet
• A chapter on public relations and the media,
including advice on planning and writing press
releases, holding news conferences and working
with the media.
• Current listings and spellings on countries and
cities around the world and a pronunciation guide
to Canadian place names
• Up-to-date information on changes to Canada's
laws on polls, elections and youth justice.
• Current advice on how to use access-to-informa-
tion laws.
• Detailed advice on writing and editing for
broadcast, dealing with the spoken word and video.

To order:
Visit thecanadianpress.com/books,
email stylebooks@thecanadianpress.com
or call 416-507-2197.

Web-based, fully searchable edition of the Stylebook and Caps and Spelling now available

All the authoritative advice on writing and editing you expect from The Canadian Press is now conveniently available at the click of a mouse through your own password-protected online account. If you prefer to use a search engine that quickly finds the content you need, instead of thumbing through an index, turn to the online stylebooks. If, instead of writing in the margins or attaching sticky notes, you prefer to create an online, searchable archive of your own notes, examples, style entries and commonly misspelled words, the online stylebooks are for you.

The stylebooks will continue to be published for hard-copy lovers, while online subscribers will benefit from:

• The convenience of using their writing resource from anywhere they have Internet access.

• The speed of real-time updates and email notifications of all style changes or additional content made by Patti Tasko, editor of the stylebooks. No more waiting for the next edition to be printed!

• The flexibility of using the basic and advanced search tools or using the intuitive links organized by popular topics, by chapter and by new entries and recent changes to the stylebooks.

• The power of searching a growing database of frequently asked questions and answers or submitting a style question directly to the editor of the stylebooks.

To sign up for an annual subscription for one or more users within your organization:

Visit thecanadianpress.com/books,
email onlinestylebooks@thecanadianpress.com
or call 416-507-2197.

Guide de rédaction – Award-winning guide for French-language writers

Winner of a prestigious award from the Office québécois de la langue française, this fifth edition – the first in almost 15 years – features:

• easy-to-follow rules for finding the right expressions and handling typographic and linguistic difficulties
• a glossary of terms and concepts in finance, law, sports and labour relations
• lists of troublesome words and common mistakes to avoid
• sections on writing about terrorism and the Canadian military
• advice on writing for and about the Internet.

To order:
Visit thecanadianpress.com/books,
email stylebooks@thecanadianpress.com
or call 416-507-2197.